A SHORT HISTORY OF

San Francisco

A SHORT HISTORY OF

San Francisco

ROBERT W. CHERNY

UNIVERSITY OF NEVADA PRESS | *Reno & Las Vegas*

University of Nevada Press | Reno, Nevada 89557 USA
www.unpress.nevada.edu

Manufactured in the United States of America

FIRST PRINTING

Cover design by Caroline Dickens
Cover photographs: iStock / Nicholas Klein

Library of Congress Cataloging-in-Publication Data

Names: Cherny, Robert W., author.
Title: A short history of San Francisco / Robert W. Cherny.
Description: Reno, Nevada: University of Nevada Press, [2026] | Includes bibliographical references. | Summary: "*A Short History of San Francisco* moves from the first Ohlone settlements to the Spanish missions and Gold Rush mansions, to the glaring inequalities of the Gilded Age and the turbulent labor politics of the early and mid-twentieth century, to the birth of the counterculture and the rise of the tech companies that now define the region."—Provided by publisher
Identifiers: LCCN 2025029898 | ISBN 9781647792251 (paperback) | ISBN 9781647792268 (ebook)
Subjects: LCSH: San Francisco (Calif.)—History. | San Francisco (Calif.)—Description and travel. | San Francisco (Calif.)—Politics and government.
Classification: LCC F869.S357 C44 2026
LC record available at https://lccn.loc.gov/2025029898

The paper used in this book meets the requirements of American National Standard for Information Sciences—Permanence of Paper for Printed Library Materials, ANSI/NISO Z39.48–1992 (R2002).

To Cerys and Sabina, San Franciscans of the twenty-first century

Contents

Illustrations

Figures

Maps

Preface and Acknowledgments

I've enjoyed living in San Francisco's Inner Sunset neighborhood for more than fifty years. My neighborhood is like a village, centered on its locally owned businesses around the intersection of 9th Avenue and Irving Street. Built up in the last years of the nineteenth century and the first few decades of the twentieth, the Inner Sunset is a mix of single-family houses, two- or three-story flats (buildings with two or three units, each with a full floor), and apartment buildings on many corners. Golden Gate Park with its Music Concourse, Botanical Garden, and Blue Heron Lake is nearby, along with the de Young Museum and California Academy of Sciences. On Sunday afternoons in the summer, the Golden Gate Park Band provides free concerts in the Music Concourse. Grandview Park, with sweeping vistas over most of the western and northern parts of the city, is also nearby.

I can walk from home to restaurants that specialize in American, Chinese, South Asian, Italian, Japanese, Mexican, Middle Eastern, Persian, Thai, or Turkish/Mediterranean cuisine, several of which feature vegetarian menus. One pizza place has remained in business for more than fifty years. My neighbors stand in line to buy baked goods at a cooperative bakery that includes a banner reading, "Make Loaves Not War." Very few neighborhood businesses are parts of national corporations.

San Francisco consists of many such neighborhoods, each a small village and each with its own distinctive characteristics. One can live in Cole Valley, Glen Park, the Inner Mission, Laurel Heights, Noe Valley, the Outer Richmond, Russian Hill, or another neighborhood and rarely venture downtown. There are, however, no agreed-upon neighborhood boundaries or even names. A Realtors' map identifies more than a hundred San Francisco neighborhoods. Even the city's Planning Department has more than one neighborhood map. In map 0.1, I've used one of the Planning Department's base maps and inserted names that are commonly used, especially those that appear in this book.

San Francisco is an incredibly beautiful city, built mostly on hills. Many neighborhoods include vistas of the downtown skyline, one or both of the great bridges, the Bay, the ocean, or several of these.

For all that diversity and variety, San Francisco is really a very small place, just forty-nine square miles. One can walk across it in a few hours—it's just over seven miles from the Bay to Ocean Beach,

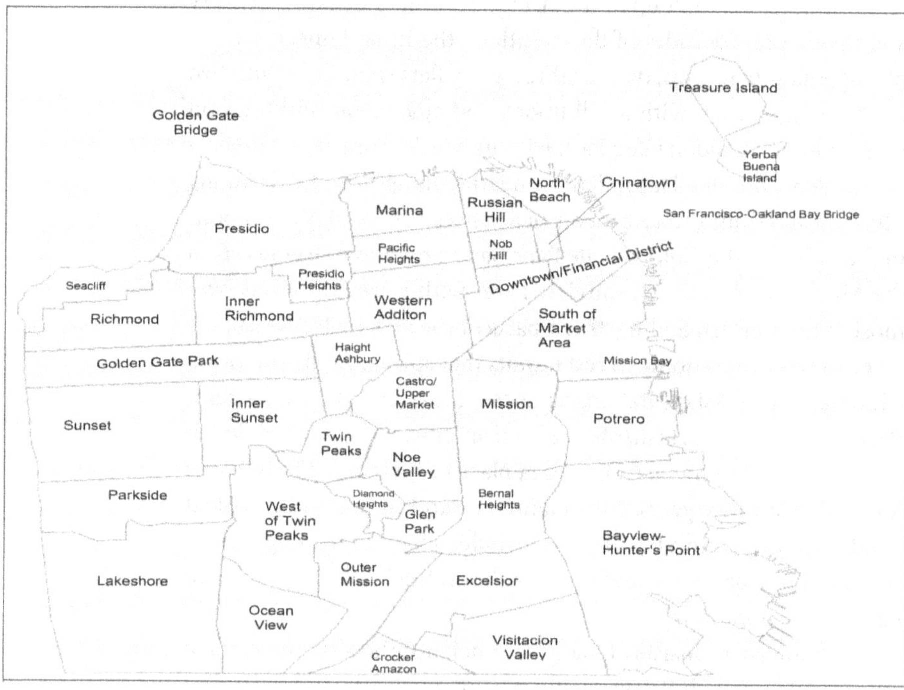

Map 0.1. There are several different ways of demarcating San Francisco's neighborhoods. This outline map is one used by the Planning Department, but a couple of the neighborhood names are not the ones used by the Planning Department. Map courtesy San Francisco Planning Department.

and it really is possible to walk across the city in most places without having to navigate around freeways, large industrial parks, or other constructed obstacles.

During the past forty-some years, I've written about aspects of San Francisco's complex and layered history—including two biographies, three monographs (one coauthored with Bill Issel), more than a dozen published essays, and articles for the Presidio Historical Association's newsletter. For nearly half my time in the city, I've been involved with historic preservation: serving on city committees and as author or coauthor of two National Register nominations, coauthor of a nomination to the Historic American Buildings Survey, and peer reviewer for several historic context statements or landmark nominations.

I am now grateful to the University of Nevada Press, especially JoAnne Banducci, Curtis Vickers, and Ryan Masteller, for this opportunity to bring much of this together, to sort out what's most significant and what's most interesting (not always the same thing), and to share what I've learned about this great city. I have, of course, drawn extensively upon nearly all my previous work, especially the published journal articles and books listed in the bibliography. Thanks especially to Bill Issel, longtime colleague and friend, for reading and offering his advice not only on this project but also on many others over the years. And thanks to Peter Richardson for his reading and thoughtful suggestions, to Bob Senkewicz for his careful reading of the first four chapters, and to Phil Faroudia, Glenna Matthews, Lorri Ungaretti, and Betty Parent, all of whom read drafts and offered suggestions. Rebekah Slonim saved me from many glitches, large and small, by her thorough copyediting. Any errors are, of course, my own.

I must also thank my family for their support and love—Rebecca, my wife and partner of fifty-eight years; Sarah, our daughter; and Cerys and Sabina, our granddaughters, to whom this book is dedicated.

A SHORT HISTORY OF

San Francisco

1

The First People

The city of San Francisco occupies the ancestral lands of the Yelamu Ramaytush Ohlone people, who lived there for thousands of years and never ceded their land to any individual, institution, or government.

Scholars once thought that the first people came to North America about 13,500 years ago, a time that coincided with the opening of a land route across the Bering Strait, called Beringia. However, recent researchers have found evidence of human presence in North America from twenty thousand years ago. Experts now assume that the process of migration to North America was an ongoing one, with some arriving over Beringia and others coming earlier, by boat, and traveling down the coast.

If the first people in the Bay Area came by boat, evidence of their presence is now underwater, because, as recently as ten thousand years ago, the shoreline was some twenty miles west of the present shoreline. What is now the Bay was then a vast meadow between the coastal ranges, with a river that ran through the canyon that is now the Golden Gate. The ocean was significantly lower because a large percentage of the earth's water was locked in giant glaciers that covered large parts of the Northern Hemisphere, although not the Pacific Coast. As the glaciers melted, beginning about ten thousand to eleven thousand years ago, the sea level rose, filling the Bay by about five thousand years ago.

San Francisco Bay became one of the most impressive natural harbors in the world, covering some four hundred square miles. Its connection to the Pacific Ocean—the Golden Gate—is so narrow that the Bay is like an inland sea, surrounded by hills. Ocean currents usually keep the area cool, with temperatures ranging between lows

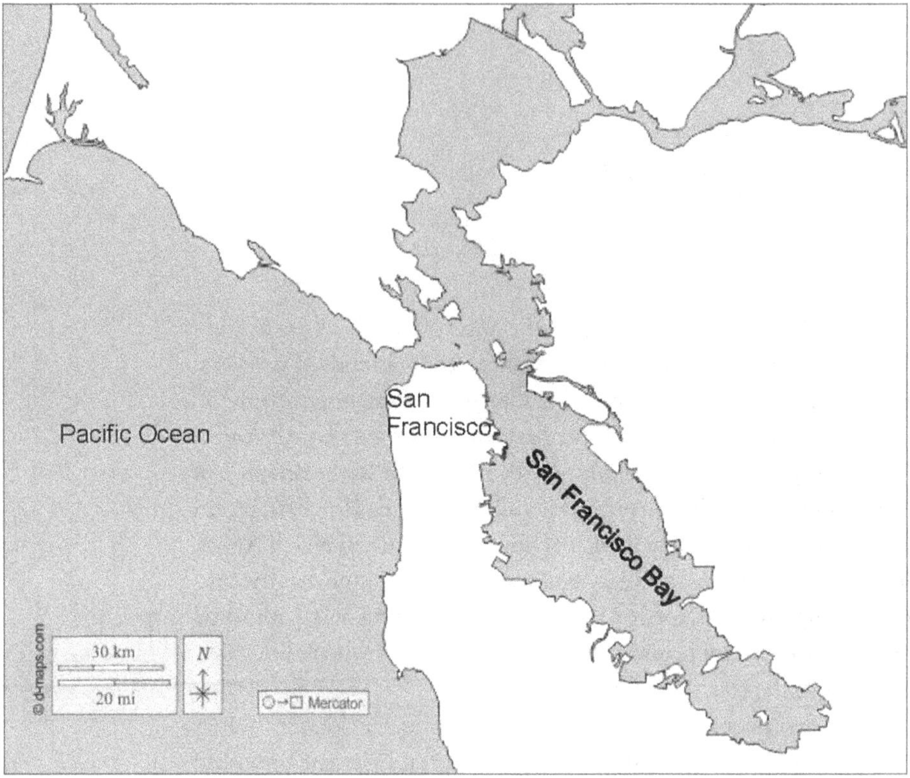

Map 1.1. The San Francisco Bay Area. Courtesy d-maps .com, Wikimedia Commons.

of 39–45 degrees Fahrenheit and highs of 72–83 degrees Fahrenheit. The same ocean currents have usually made for rainy winters and cool but dry summers.

Archaeological evidence suggests the presence of humans in the Bay Area by ten thousand years ago and a continuing presence by six thousand years ago. Archaeological evidence also suggests that the ancestors of the Ohlone were in the Bay Area by at least 4,500 years ago, and DNA evidence confirms their presence 2,000 years ago.

The Ohlone language is part of the Penutian language group, found mostly in Central and Northern California, and is related to languages spoken by peoples in the Pacific Northwest. Scholars surmise that the ancestors of the Ohlone may have arrived by boat or on foot, but the Ohlone people had a different account of their origin.

COYOTE, EAGLE, HUMMINGBIRD, AND THE ORIGIN OF THE OHLONE PEOPLE

In 1901, Alfred Kroeber became the first person appointed to the anthropology faculty at the University of California. Over the following years, he interviewed members of California Indigenous tribes about the stories that had been passed down from their elders. He was unable to locate any from the Ramaytush Ohlone, but he was given this account by one of the Rumsen Ohlone people, who lived in the vicinity of what is now Monterey.

"When this world was finished, the eagle, the humming-bird, and Coyote were standing on the top of Pico Blanco. When the water rose to their feet, the eagle, carrying the humming-bird and Coyote, flew to the Sierra de Gabilan. There they stood until the water went down. Then the eagle sent Coyote down the mountain to see if the world were dry. Coyote came back and said: 'The whole world is dry.' The eagle said to him: 'Go and look in the river. See what is there.' Coyote came back and said: 'There is a beautiful girl.' The eagle said: 'She will be your wife in order that people may be raised again.' . . . [Coyote's descendants became the Ohlone.] Coyote gave the people the carrying net. He gave them bow and arrows to kill rabbits. He said: 'You will have acorn mush for your food. You will gather acorns and you will have acorn bread to eat.'"

The Ohlone established villages on what is now the San Francisco Peninsula, the eastern and southern sides of the Bay, and down the coast to the Monterey area, eventually developing into five dialect regions. Spanish colonizers called them *Costeños*, or people of the coast. Later anthropologists adapted that name as Costanoans. Today they are usually called Ohlone, which is what they called themselves and what their descendants today prefer. In the Ohlone language, *Ramaytush* means people from the west, as distinguished from the Ohlone of the East Bay.

In 1776, when the Spanish arrived, the Ramaytush Ohlone were divided into several groups by dialect and geographic area. The Yelamu lived at the north end of the peninsula, in roughly the area of modern San Francisco, in several villages, each consisting of several families. Each village had a traditional area within which village members moved from season to season. Most lived in what is now the southeastern quarter of San Francisco, but one village, Petlenuc, was located on the north side of the peninsula and another, Ompuromo, was near the south end of what is now Lake Merced.

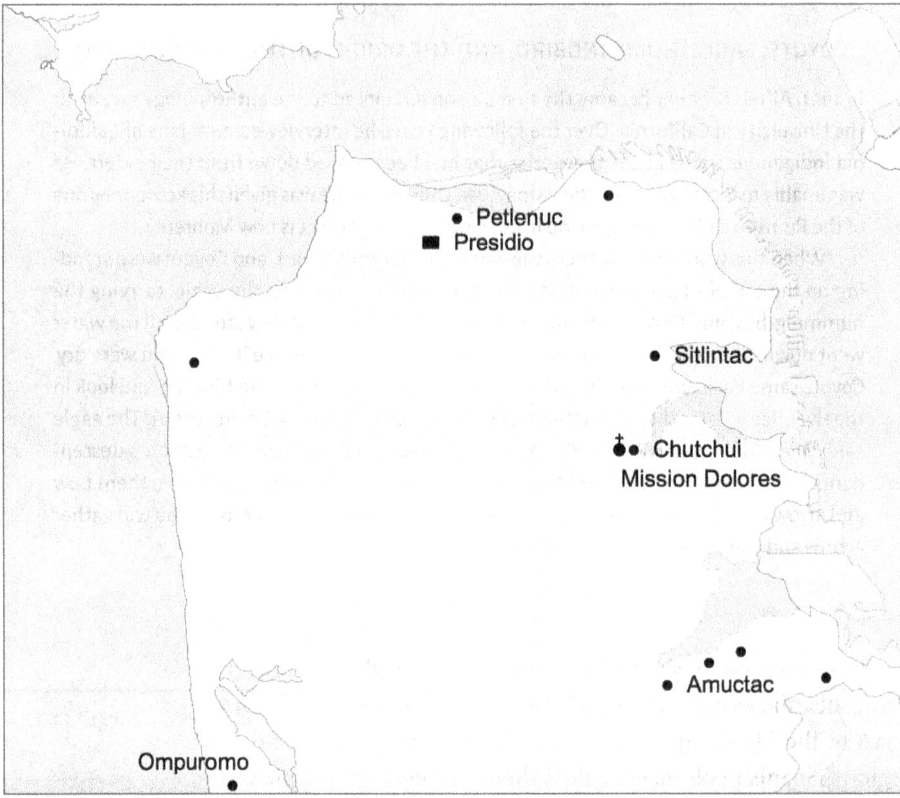

Map 1.2. This map identifies the locations of the major Yelamu villages as of 1776 when the Spanish arrived, and also the locations of the two major Spanish settlements, the Mission and the Presidio. Note, too, the location of the original shoreline as compared with the current shoreline. Yelamu map courtesy Noahedits, Wikimedia Commons.

All the Yelamu villages were near fresh water and all but one were on the Bay. The people were hunter-gatherers, subsisting on shellfish, fish, marine and land mammals, birds, eggs, grass seeds, and acorns. Acorns were a major staple. Like many other Native California peoples, the Ohlone managed meadowlands through burning, which enriched the soil and helped the germination of the grasses they harvested for seeds. Burning also kept meadows from becoming forests, which meant that grazing deer and elk were easier to hunt.

Figure 1.1. Louis Choris created the original of this image of three Ohlone in a tule-reed canoe in 1816 when he was in the area with the Russian ship *Rurik*. His original image was turned into the lithograph you see here in 1822. The person in the middle seems to be wearing a blanket woven of wool, likely created at the Mission. When Anton Refregier created his murals at Rincon Annex in the 1940s (see p. 106), he used this image as the basis for one of his murals. Choris/Victor Adam, "Bateau du port de San Francisco" (boat of San Francisco Bay), *Voyage pittoresque autour du monde* (1822), fG420.K84.C6 1822 VAULT pt. 3, pl. 10, courtesy the Bancroft Library, University of California, Berkeley.

Ohlone women made elaborate baskets that fulfilled many functions. Some baskets were woven so tightly that they held water and were used for cooking: acorn flour was mixed with water and heated by placing hot stones in the basket. Other baskets were used for carrying, storage, and catching fish. Baskets often featured elaborate designs unique to a particular village or individual basket-maker.

The Ohlone's housing was simple but well suited to the environment. They used tree branches or saplings to construct a conical frame that they covered with brush or reeds. Tule reeds were also used to make canoes that they used for fishing, transportation, and trading expeditions around the Bay.

As was the case with nearly all the Indigenous peoples of North and Mesoamerica, Ohlone villages included a sweat lodge, where men smoked tobacco and conducted spiritual ceremonies. The Ohlone saw all living things as having a spirit. They believed in an afterlife in which their spirit went to another land across the sea. Immediately after death, the corpse was cremated.

Outside each Ohlone village was a huge shell mound, which developed over millennia, consisting not only of shells but also bones, including the bones of their dead. Ceremonial fires were sometimes lit on top of shell mounds. In 1909, an anthropologist counted some 425 shell mounds around the Bay, including two large ones in the northwestern part of what is now San Francisco and several in the southeastern area. Many of these shell mounds were subsequently destroyed, but the Ohlone today consider surviving shell mounds to be sacred places.

Archaeologists understand that the Ohlone people's way of life evolved over the thousands of years that they lived around the San Francisco Bay. But those patterns of life were first challenged and then forever changed by the arrival of Spanish colonizers in 1776.

2

Mission and Presidio

Spanish Colonial Outpost, 1776–1822

In 1776, while English colonists on the other side of North America were declaring their independence from Britain, a Spanish expedition was establishing a mission and presidio (military post) in the far northern reaches of New Spain, in what is now San Francisco. Those institutions spelled the end of the independence of the Ohlone.

Spanish colonizers came to the Bay Area more than two hundred years after they first arrived in North America. Between 1519 and 1521, Spanish forces conquered what is today central Mexico. By 1600, they ruled a huge colonial empire. New Spain eventually included what is now Mexico, most of Central America, and the southwestern United States. Missions and presidios were two of the most significant institutions for this expansion.

Spain colonized the Bay Area only in the late 1700s, primarily because of events remote from the region. New Spain included the Philippine Islands. Most contact between Spain and the Philippines took place across the Pacific, avoiding the colonial outposts of other, sometimes hostile, European powers. Once a year, in Manila, a galleon was filled with luxury goods from East Asia and sent across the Pacific, following the prevailing currents and coming to land near what is now Mendocino, California. The galleons then followed the coast south to Acapulco, where they were unloaded and their goods transported overland to be sent by ship to Spain.

In the 1760s, fearing that British and Russian expansion in North America could threaten the Manila galleons, Spanish authorities sought to extend their control along the Alta (upper, as opposed to Baja, lower) California coast by creating ports, missions, and presidios.

In 1769–70, the Portola expedition established ports at San Diego and Monterey. Some members of the expedition continued north and, in 1769, became the first Europeans to see—and name—San Francisco Bay, which one of them estimated was large enough to hold all the navies of Europe. In 1776, a colonizing expedition arrived at what is now San Francisco.

Throughout the Spanish Empire in the Americas, missions were considered to be transitional institutions, intended to transform the lives of the Indigenous people by converting them to Christianity and assimilating them into Spanish life. Once the assimilation was complete, the mission lands would be turned over to the assimilated people, who would form towns (pueblos) and live as farmers and ranchers. That ideal was never realized.

A SPANISH PRIEST VIEWS SAN FRANCISCO BAY, 1776

Pedro Font, a Catholic priest, was part of the Spanish exploring party in 1776 that selected the site for the first Spanish settlements in what is now San Francisco. He recorded his observations in his diary:

> *Wednesday, March 27*—I said Mass. In the morning the weather was fair and very clear, a favor which God granted us during all these days, and especially today, in order that we might see the harbor which we were going to explore . . . The port [that is, bay] of San Francisco . . . is a marvel of nature, and might well be called the harbor of harbors, because of its great capacity . . .
>
> *Thursday, March 28*—I said Mass. . . . [Later] we ascended a small hill and then entered upon a mesa that was very green and flower-covered, with an abundance of wild violets. . . . This mesa affords a most delightful view . . . Indeed, although in my travels I saw very good sites and beautiful country, I saw none which pleased me so much as this. And I think that if it could be well settled like Europe there would not be anything more beautiful in all the world, for it has the best advantages for founding in it a most beautiful city, with all the conveniences desired, by land as well as by sea with that harbor so remarkable and so spacious, in which may be established shipyards, docks, and anything that might be wished.

Few Indigenous people came to the Alta California missions voluntarily. Some came out of curiosity and were converted without fully understanding what they had done. Once baptized, they became "neophytes" (newly baptized people) and were subject to the authority of the missionaries, who regulated their lives in an effort to make them fully assimilated members of the Christian community. If they ran away, soldiers from the nearest presidio tried to find them and bring them back. Sometimes the soldiers seized any Indigenous people they could find—whether runaways or not. Once a mission had enough neophytes to create a surplus of food, it attracted those who needed food. For some, conversion to Christianity became a way to gain food and shelter.

The mission established on San Francisco Bay in 1776, the sixth in Alta California, was located near a large Ohlone village in what is now the Mission District. Officially Misión San Francisco de Asís, it has long been called Mission Dolores after a nearby creek and lake (now vanished) named for Nuestra Señora de los Dolores, "Our Lady of Sorrows"—Mary, the mother of Jesus. Mission Dolores developed slowly. No convert was baptized for nearly a year. The current church building, now the oldest intact church nave in California, was constructed between 1788 and 1791 through the labor of the Indigenous converts. In 2004, a large original mural painted by those laborers was discovered behind the wooden altar that was shipped from Mexico and installed in 1796. Other buildings housed the priests and the neophytes or were used for agriculture or manufacturing.

By 1801, all the Indigenous people of the San Francisco Peninsula had become part of the community centered on Mission Dolores. Other Indigenous people from around the Bay, including Miwoks, Patwins, and Wappos, also came to Mission Dolores. Over the following years, these groups intermarried. As of 1820, the Mission counted thousands of converts. They found mission life very different from their earlier lives. Some tried to escape. In 1796, for example, almost one quarter of the nearly nine hundred neophytes ran away. The death rate at Mission Dolores was the highest of all the missions. Some five thousand Indigenous people had died at Mission Dolores by the time the Mission closed. They died from European diseases but also, it seems, from the emotional and physical consequences of losing their previous lives. By 1834, when the process of closing the Mission began, the community there included only thirty-seven descendants of the original Ohlone groups who had once lived on the peninsula. It was long thought that the last known descendent of the Ohlone people of the peninsula died in the 1920s. However, a few individuals have recently traced their ancestry to Ohlone who were baptized at Mission Dolores.

At its fullest development, between 1810 and 1822, the Mission housed some 1,100–1,200 neophytes who farmed and ranched. By 1810, they tended eleven thousand sheep, eleven thousand head of cattle, and thousands of horses, mules, goats, and pigs. The fields and pasture (*potrero*) of the Mission occupied most of what is today the southeastern quarter of the city. The neophytes also manufactured woolen goods, using twenty looms to make cloth from the wool of the Mission's sheep.

Figure 2.1. An unknown artist's representation of Mission Dolores in 1830. From John W. Dwinelle, *The Colonial History of the City of San Francisco*, 3rd ed., p. 149, photo courtesy the British Library on Flicker Commons.

Though Mission Dolores became a successful agricultural and manufacturing operation, the Presidio of San Francisco, also founded in 1776, was slow to develop. Located at the northern end of the peninsula, the purpose of the Presidio was to defend the Bay against foreign ships, protect the Mission, and track down and return escaping neophytes. Throughout most of its existence, it was the northernmost of the Spanish presidios.

The Presidio never developed as a fortress by European standards, nor even by comparison to presidios further south. When George Vancouver, a British explorer, visited in 1792, he described it as poorly fortified and "resembling a [com]pound for cattle." A drawing from that expedition shows a U-shaped collection of adobe buildings with a fence of brush as the fourth wall. It was, Vancouver thought, very different from "the ideas we had conceived of the sumptuous manner in which Spaniards live on this side of the globe." He also considered it easy to conquer. The year after Vancouver's visit, and perhaps inspired by that visit, construction began on the Castillo de San Joaquin, a fortification where Fort Point now stands, overlooking the Golden Gate and equipped with ten cannon.

Perhaps the best known episode in the history of the Presidio is the romantic, and often romanticized, story of Count Nikolai Rezanov and Concepción Argüello, the daughter of the Presidio's *comandante*. Rezanov arrived in the Bay in 1806, seeking to barter for food for the Russian settlements in what is now Alaska. Though he was forty-two and she was fifteen, the two supposedly fell in love, but marriage had to wait until he could return from a trip to Russia, where he had to go to request permission to marry a Catholic. He died crossing Siberia, but years passed before she learned of his death. She vowed that she would marry no other man, later moved with her parents to Southern California, and devoted her life to pious works and helping the unfortunate. In 1851, she became the first Catholic nun in California.

In October 1816, the *Rurik*, an Imperial Russian ship on a voyage of exploration, entered San Francisco Bay and remained for several weeks. The expedition included two naturalists and an artist, whose accounts of the area and its people provide important early sources about the area at that time.

The expedition's botanist, Adelbert von Chamisso, kept a journal in which he described their arrival in the Bay: "A great deal of movement in the fort [the Presidio] at the southern entrance of the channel was apparent. They hoisted their flag; we hoisted ours, which did not seem to be recognized, and saluted the Spanish by firing seven times. . . . We anchored before the Presidio, but no boat started from the shore to us, since the Spaniards did not possess a single boat."

While in the Bay Area, the expedition's naturalists described more than thirty new plant species including the California poppy, to which Chamisso gave its scientific name, *Eschscholzia californica*, in honor of the ship's doctor, Johann Friedrich von Eschscholtz. In return, Eschscholtz named a local lupine species, *Lupinus chamissonis*, in honor of Chamisso. Both names remain the scientific names of those California native plants.

The expedition's artist, Louis Choris, made drawings and watercolors, later converted to lithographs, that provide some of the earliest images of the Presidio and the Mission of San Francisco (see portfolio A). Choris depicted the Presidio structures as enclosing all four sides of an open square, unlike the 1792 drawing. He spent considerable time drawing at the Mission, including attending a dance by a visiting group of Indigenous people who lived outside the mission system. One member of the *Rurik*'s crew wrote the notation for the music for the dance, the first known recording of California Indigenous music. Subsequent artists have drawn upon Choris's work depicting the people of the Presidio and Mission at the beginning of the nineteenth century.

Assessment of the missions is a contested topic. Early evaluations praised them for bringing Christianity and European culture to the Indigenous peoples. There is consensus today that the missionaries intended to assimilate the Indians—turn them into model Spanish peasants. Sympathetic accounts today emphasize the priests' religious devotion to the conversion and spiritual welfare of their flock, but others condemn them for creating a form of bound labor just short of slavery. Throughout Spanish America, flogging was the basic form of punishment. Missionaries meted out this harsh punishment, although the beatings were generally administered by soldiers from

A RUSSIAN VISITOR CRITICIZES THE MISSIONARIES, 1816

Adelbert von Chamisso was a botanist, born in France and raised in Germany. He was a member of the *Rurik* expedition that visited the Presidio and Mission in 1816. He recorded his observations of the Mission in his diary:

> The pious Franciscans who maintain the missions in new California are not trained in any of the arts and crafts that they are supposed to practice and teach here nor in any of the languages that the peoples to which they are sent speak. . . . The Indian himself does not draw any direct profit from his labor and no wages if, for instance, he is rented out as a day laborer to the Presidio. . . . We do not deny the gentleness, the paternal care of the missionaries. . . . But the relationship remains the one described and would, it seems to us, be different only in name if a slaveholder kept them for labor and rented them out at will.

Chamisso also wrote about the soldiers of the Presidio:

> The misery in which they [the soldiers] languished, forgotten and deserted for six or seven years by Mexico, their motherland, did not permit them to be hosts . . . They spoke with bitterness of the missionaries, who . . . deliver to them nothing without a requisition, and even then only that which was absolutely indispensable to their sustenance . . . A soldier . . . complained to us that the Commandant would not permit them to press [impress into service] natives from the opposite shore, in order to force them to work for the soldiers, as they did in the missions.

the Presidio. Many of the priests also practiced self-flagellation, believing that by inflicting pain on themselves they could better participate in the suffering of Christ. Such attitudes and beliefs were a product of their culture, in which the soul was considered more important than the body and severe punishments were the norm. The mission fathers, as a group, were not vicious, if judged by the culture in which they lived. They surely did not intend the high death rate at the Mission. However, their critics point out that the missionaries' heavy-handed efforts at assimilation constituted cultural genocide, an effort to destroy the Indians' own culture and replace it with that of Spain. Mariano Guadalupe Vallejo, born in Monterey in 1807 and later a high-ranking military officer in Spanish and Mexican California, was highly critical of the missionaries, later observing that it would have been "disadvantageous" to "the Missionary Fathers" for "their pupils [to] become enlightened and claim they deserved to be treated as intelligent human beings."

By 1816, when the *Rurik* visited the Bay, the Presidio and Mission were entering their final years. A revolution in Mexico in 1810 initiated eleven years of armed conflict. Negotiations finally brought Mexican independence in 1821. During those years, Spanish authorities in Mexico City concentrated their resources in central New Spain, rather than on the far northern frontier.

Both the Mission and the Presidio were soon abandoned.

PORTFOLIO A

Life at the Mission, 1816

The Art of Louis Choris

Louis Choris did extensive drawing and painting with watercolors during the visit of the Russian ship *Rurik* to San Francisco Bay in 1816. Later, in Paris, Victor Adam converted Choris's drawings and paintings to lithographs, many of which were hand-colored, and published them as a book in 1822, titled *Voyage pittoresque autour du monde* (Scenic journey around the world). Today, the lithographs are the best known version of Choris's works; Choris's original works and the lithographs provide the earliest known visual depictions of life at the Mission.

All of Choris's pictures of life at Mission Dolores include Indigenous people. Some Native Californians today object to the use of such depictions by a European. Comparing Choris's originals with the later lithographs suggests that the lithographs sometimes—even frequently—presented the Native Californians as darker and more exotic than Choris's original works. Scholars today understand that race is a social construct, and that most Europeans in the early nineteenth century constructed people in other parts of the world as exotic others—not only different in culture but also darker in color and culturally inferior. Despite these limitations, Choris's works remain our earliest visual depictions of life in what became San Francisco.

Figure A.1. Choris labeled this original drawing, in French, as "Costumes of the war dance of the inhabitants of California in the vicinity of Mission of San Francisco." His notes identify the two men as Olompoli and Sactan. Choris, *Costumes de danse de guerre des habitants de la Californie du voisinage de la mission de Sn. Francisco*, ca. 1816, drawing on paper, watercolor 27.5 x 23 cm., Robert B. Honeyman, Jr. Collection of Early Californian and Western American Pictorial Material, BANC PIC 1963.002:1313 (recto)—FR, photograph courtesy of the Bancroft Library, University of California, Berkeley.

Figure A.2. This is another of Choris's watercolors. Louis Choris, "Indian of California," ca. 1816, watercolor on paper, object identification number A55.20.1, photograph courtesy Oakland Museum of California.

Figure A.3. This lithograph of the dance scene and Choris's original watercolor on which it is based are the earliest visual representations of the Mission buildings. The two missionaries on the left side do not appear in Choris's original; otherwise, the two are virtually identical. The caption of the lithograph translates as "Dance of the inhabitants of California at the mission of San Francisco." Louis Choris/Victor Adam, "Danse des habitants de la Californie à la mission de San Francisco," *Voyage pittoresque autour du monde* (1822), Robert B. Honeyman, Jr. Collection of Early Californian and Western American Pictorial Material, BANC PIC 1963.002:1312—FR, photograph courtesy the Bancroft Library, University of California, Berkeley.

Figure A.4. The translation of the title of this lithograph is "The game of the habitants of California in the mission of San Francisco." The "game" is likely a form of gambling, a practice that predated the arrival of the missionaries. This suggests that, despite the efforts of the missionaries, some—likely many—previous practices persisted among the neophytes. Louis Choris/Victor Adam, "Jeux des habitants de la Californie à la mission de San Francisco," *Voyage pittoresque autour du monde* (1822), digitized by Getty Research Institute, courtesy the Internet Archive.

3

Pueblo and Ranchos

Mexican San Francisco, 1822–46

Mexicans' struggle for independence from Spain began in 1810, but independence came only in 1821, with the Treaty of Córdoba. The usual date for the beginning of Mexican California is 1822, when the first Mexican governor was appointed. What is now San Francisco remained one of the most remote outposts of the new nation. The major population centers of Alta California were to the south, especially San Diego, Los Angeles, and Monterey.

By 1820 or so, more than forty years had passed since the first Spanish settlers arrived in Alta California, and their descendants had begun to develop a regional identity and call themselves "Californios." Between 1810 and 1822, Californios became accustomed to running their own affairs, without interference from Mexico City. After 1822, California's political situation became more complicated as a succession of governors faced repeated conspiracies and rebellions, and the governorship often seemed a revolving door.

The years when Mexico governed—or attempted to govern—Alta California included major changes for what is now San Francisco. The first major change was secularization. The intent of secularization was to break up the mission system and convert the missions' lands into pueblos—villages of Hispanicized Indigenous people. Authorities in Mexico City wanted to end the Spanish system of large landholding missions and replace them with "secular" parishes. These new parishes were to include the church structure itself, but not the extensive mission lands. The secularization of Mission Dolores resulted in the creation of ranchos, the decline of the Presidio, and the development of the Pueblo of Yerba Buena as a port.

The governor began the process of secularization in 1826 with a decree of partial emancipation, specifying that Indians could leave the missions if they had been Christians since childhood or for fifteen years, were married, and were able to earn their living. However, many of the Californios wanted the missions' lands for themselves. And mission lands were granted by the governor to local Californios, creating an aristocracy of landed families. Many homeless Christianized Indigenous people went to work for the Californios who took over the mission lands, becoming vaqueros (cowboys), domestic servants, and laborers. Others left the areas settled by Californios.

In 1834, secularization reached Mission Dolores. Except for the church, the residence of the priests, and a small amount of surrounding land, everything else was secularized. By 1842, there were only eight Indigenous people still living at the Mission. All of the Mission's pastures, farmland, and other possessions were turned over to an administrator. The last priest left in 1845. Though Mission Dolores was virtually abandoned, a settlement grew up around it, made up of Californios and the assimilated Indigenous people who worked for them.

Much of what is now San Francisco was handed out as land grants by the governor. Under Mexican law, the usual way an individual

Figure 3.1. Mission Dolores in 1856. Photograph by Carleton Watkins, courtesy California State Library.

obtained a rancho was to file a petition with the governor requesting a defined piece of land, described in general terms and accompanied by a crude map. If the governor approved and there were no conflicting interests, a formal grant was made. Any livestock roaming the area were usually part of the grant.

As was true elsewhere in Alta California, nearly all those who received ranchos in what is now San Francisco were members of influential families. Several held local political positions. In 1835, José Antonio Galindo, a corporal at the Presidio of San Francisco and a third-generation Californio, was granted the Rancho Laguna de la Merced in what is now southwestern San Francisco and northwestern San Mateo County; he soon sold it to Francisco de Haro. In 1839, members of the Peralta family were granted the Rancho Potrero de San Francisco, once part of the *potrero* or pasture of the Mission. In 1845, José de Jesus Noe was granted much of the remaining mission lands as the Rancho San Miguel, located in the center of what is now San Francisco and comprising about one-sixth of the modern city's land area. A few grant recipients were Anglo newcomers who converted to Catholicism and became Mexican citizens to be eligible for a land grant. Jacob Leese, born in Ohio, came to California in 1833. He converted to Catholicism, became a Mexican citizen, and married the sister of Mariano Guadalupe Vallejo, *comandante* of the Presidio of San Francisco and a significant political figure in Alta California. Leese received a large land grant in what is now southeastern San Francisco and northeastern San Mateo County.

Ranchos were also established on mission lands in what is now Marin and Sonoma Counties, north of the Bay. The largest went to Vallejo. Concerned about Fort Ross, established by the Russians on the coast sixty miles from the village of Sonoma, Vallejo ordered most soldiers to move from the San Francisco Presidio to Sonoma. By 1835, only a few caretakers remained at the Presidio.

In 1834, Vallejo received official approval from the governor to create a pueblo near Yerba Buena Cove, in the northeastern part of the peninsula, the best place for ships to anchor and transfer cargo to and from the shore. A town was laid out around a plaza, now Portsmouth Square. Francisco de Haro was elected as the first alcalde, a

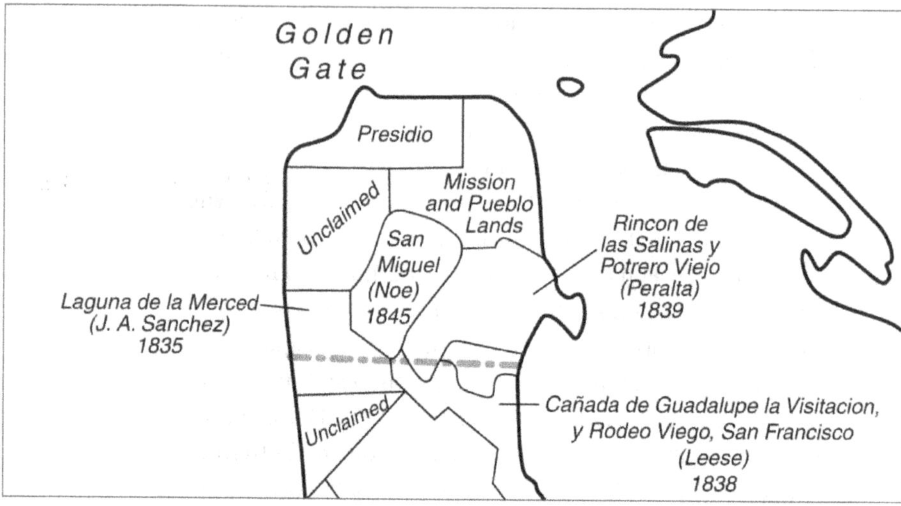

Map 3.1. Map of ranchos in what is now San Francisco, ca. 1845. No one was interested in most of the western part of the city, which consisted almost entirely of sand dunes. Map adapted from figure 14, "Spanish and Mexican Period Ranchos of San Francisco and San Mateo Counties," in Randall Milliken et al., *Ohlone/Costanoan Indians of the San Francisco Peninsula and Their Neighbors, Yesterday and Today* (2009), courtesy Randall Milliken et al., and National Park Service, Golden Gate National Recreation Area.

position similar to both mayor and justice of the peace. A six-member *ayuntamiento*, or council, was also elected, consisting of members of other prominent families. When most of the Presidio's troops moved to Sonoma, some of the Presidio families moved to the Pueblo of Yerba Buena. By the late 1830s, what is now San Francisco included a settlement around the old mission, a few mostly deserted buildings at the Presidio, and the beginnings of a village at Yerba Buena Cove.

William Richardson, a British subject, had converted to Catholicism, become a Mexican citizen, and married into a local Californio family. Under his leadership, Yerba Buena became the major port north of Monterey. In 1837, a total of twenty-five ships came to Yerba Buena, ten of them from the United States, to unload manufactured goods and take on hides and tallow, produced by the ranchos around the Bay and in demand by the factories of New England for the production of leather products and candles. Some rancho owners grew

M. G. VALLEJO SMUGGLES BANNED BOOKS THROUGH THE PORT OF YERBA BUENA, 1831

Yerba Buena became an officially recognized port, but civil and religious authorities sought to restrict what might be imported. Mariano Guadalupe Vallejo, who was literate in English, French, and Latin as well as Spanish, left this reminiscence about how he was able to acquire his library.

"The Reverend Missionary Fathers were staunchly opposed to our having access to any books that could tend to influence our thinking in terms of liberal ideas and awareness of the rights of free men. . . . In 1831 the Mexican merchant frigate *Leonor* arrived at the port of San Francisco. The supercargo and owner of the ship . . . agreed to sell a large collection of books to me . . . The authorities quickly took the necessary steps to have the books confiscated. . . . Fortunately, I found out what was being plotted . . . In exchange for 400 [cattle] hides and ten barrels of lard [tallow], I became the owner of the best library that had existed in Las Californias up to that point. . . . My friends and I hungered to know what men of science and intelligence in the Old World were writing about and thinking. . . . My soul was bursting with joy and satisfaction."

Vallejo shared his library with his closest friends. When religious authorities found out about the books, Vallejo and his friends were briefly excommunicated. Vallejo later recalled that the excommunication was lifted with one restriction: Vallejo and his friends had permission to read "all types of books," but "they were not to allow the works of Rousseau and Voltaire to fall into the hands of people with little intelligence, since those works would undoubtedly undermine their religious convictions."

wealthy from the hide and tallow trade. Not all the visiting ships came to trade. Some whaling ships, many also from New England, were interested in buying provisions—food and fresh water. Juana Briones and her children moved from the Presidio area, created a home near the new plaza, and profited from selling provisions to visiting ships.

Many Californios were dissatisfied with the remote Mexican government and had deposed several Mexican governors. A successful rebellion in 1836 had increased their self-confidence that they could control their own affairs. By the mid-1840s, some of them, notably Vallejo, began to talk about separating from Mexico and joining the United States. However, that event came without any initiative from the Californios, and over the objections of many of them.

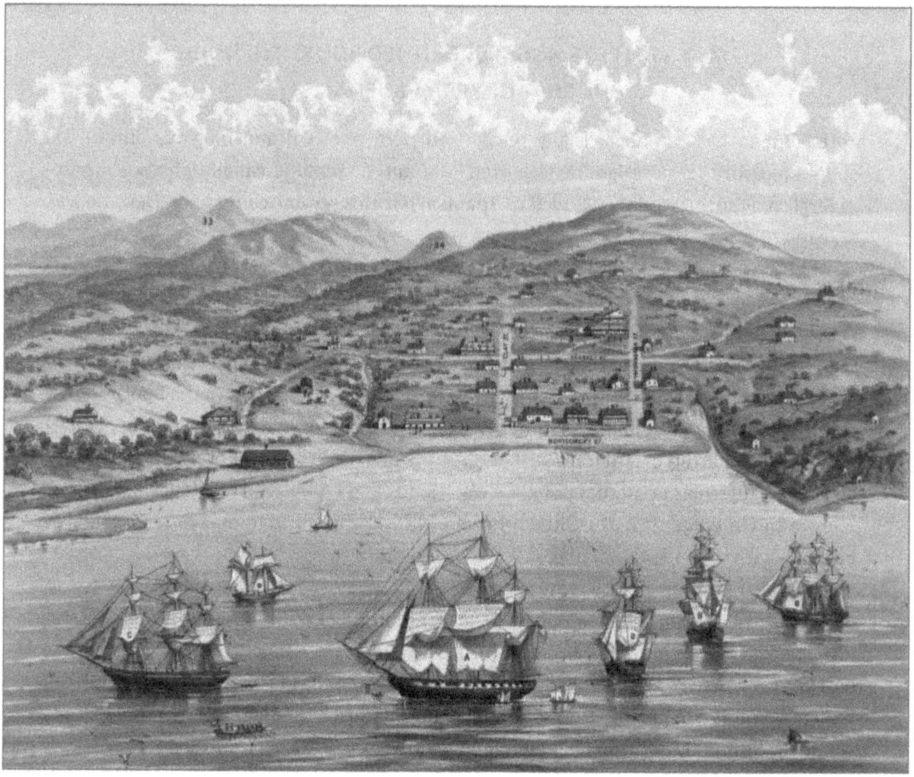

Figure 3.2. An artist's recreation of the Pueblo of Yerba Buena ca. 1847, published in 1884. The largest building, behind the flagpole, was the customs house, the major governmental center. "View of San Francisco, formerly Yerba Buena, before the discovery of gold," Bosqui Eng. & Print. Co., 1884, courtesy the Library of Congress, Geography and Map Division.

4

Instant City

War, Gold, and Crisis, 1846–65

In early June 1846, the US Navy ship *Portsmouth* sailed into San Francisco Bay and stopped first at the village of Sausalito, across the bay from Yerba Buena. William Richardson came on board to pilot the ship to Yerba Buena Cove. On July 9, Captain John Montgomery and some of his crew came ashore at Yerba Buena, lowered the Mexican flag at the plaza, and raised the US flag. Mexico and the United States were at war, and California was the great prize in the contest. The plaza was soon renamed for the *Portsmouth*.

War

Beginning in the 1830s, American presidents had tried repeatedly to purchase California from Mexico. They were especially interested in the Bay Area, the best potential port on the Pacific Coast. Mexico refused to sell. In 1845, President James Polk again offered to purchase California, and the Mexican government again refused. Texas became a state that year, but the Mexican government did not accept the Rio Grande as the southern boundary of Texas. In the spring of 1846, Mexican troops skirmished with US troops in the disputed territory. Claiming Mexico had invaded the United States, Polk asked Congress to declare war, offering as one justification that the Mexican government had refused to sell California. On May 13, 1846, Congress voted to declare war on Mexico. There was significant opposition to the war in the North, where opponents of slavery viewed it as a conspiracy by slave owners. Some, including Abraham Lincoln and Henry David Thoreau, came to oppose the war on moral grounds, because they considered the United States to be the aggressor.

Polk had dispatched US naval forces to the California coast before requesting a declaration of war. When US forces landed at Yerba Buena, they encountered no opposition. They took charge of the city, and Captain Montgomery appointed Lieutenant Washington Bartlett as the new alcalde.

Soon after, on July 31, the passenger ship *Brooklyn* arrived in the Bay carrying some two hundred Mormons, led by Sam Brannan. They had left the Eastern US before the war began, intending to travel overland from Yerba Buena to the Mormon settlement in what is now Utah, with the goal of getting far outside the US, where they had been repeatedly attacked and their leader murdered. Given the new situation, Brannan and many of the Mormons remained in Yerba Buena, doubling the population of the village. In January 1847, Brannan established the town's first newspaper, the *California Star*. Soon after, Alcalde Bartlett published a notice renaming the town San Francisco, identifying it with the Bay.

The key military actions of the war took place in and near Mexico City, and the war was over relatively quickly. In February 1848, the Treaty of Guadalupe Hidalgo formally transferred Mexico's provinces of Alta California and Nuevo Mexico—55 percent of the land area of Mexico—and the US paid Mexico $15 million. The military conquest of California had proceeded quickly. The cultural conquest of Northern California was also very rapid, once the news reached the Eastern US and the rest of the world that gold had been discovered near Sacramento.

Gold

A month before the treaty, in January 1848, workers near Sacramento discovered gold. When Sam Brannan learned about it, he ran through the streets of San Francisco, shouting, "Gold, Gold from the American River," setting off the Gold Rush. Thousands of goldseekers descended on San Francisco, most arriving by ship, coming from the Eastern US, Europe, Australia, Latin America—especially the mining areas of northern Mexico and Chile—and elsewhere in the world. Ships clogged the cove, many of them abandoned as their

Figure 4.1. William Shew took this daguerreotype in 1852, showing Yerba Buena Cove and adjacent parts of San Francisco Bay clogged with ships, some of them abandoned as their passengers and crews both hastened to the goldfields. Courtesy the National Museum of American History.

crews joined the rush to the Gold Country, the western slope of the Sierra Nevada, 130 miles east of San Francisco.

By mid-1849, the population of this instant city reached about five thousand. In 1860, it reached fifty thousand, making it the fifteenth-largest city in the nation. The city first consisted of tents, hastily constructed shacks, abandoned ships, and only a few well-built structures, all highly susceptible to fire. Devastating fires in the 1850s led city authorities to adopt the city's first building code, which prohibited canvas and cloth buildings anywhere and banned wooden buildings in a "fire district" centered on the emerging central business district.

In 1859, after the city had been repeatedly rebuilt after major fires, civic leaders adopted a city seal featuring a phoenix, a legendary bird reborn from fire. The shield, depicting a ship passing through the Golden Gate, is flanked by a miner holding a shovel and a sailor holding a sextant, symbolizing mining and commerce. The motto is

Figure 4.2. The San Francisco City Seal. Source: City and County of San Francisco.

in Spanish: *Oro en paz, fierro en guerra* (Gold in peace, iron in war). However, as it turned out soon after, it was gold that was the city's and state's major contribution during the Civil War.

Given the influx of so many thousands, California qualified for statehood in 1850 without passing through territorial status. The first state legislature gave the instant city a charter that established its boundaries and form of government. At first, San Francisco County included both San Francisco and what is now San Mateo County. Subsequent legislatures changed the city's boundaries and modified its government. In 1856, the legislature passed the Consolidation Act, which created California's only combined city and county government, the City and County of San Francisco, with the Board of Supervisors as its legislative body. The Consolidation Act also created San Mateo County.

The Crisis of the 1850s

In the 1850s, the new city and the nation were experiencing separate crises of political legitimacy. At the national level the crisis was over slavery. The two sides, northern abolitionists and southern slave owners, denied each other's legitimacy, and both cited their devotion to the highest principles. The Mexican war and acquisition of extensive new territory threatened the previous, delicate balance between states that permitted slavery and states that prohibited it. The California constitution, in 1850, prohibited slavery, and admission of California as a free state upset the even balance between slave states and free states. The compromise that admitted California included the Fugitive Slave Act, committing the federal government to assist efforts to capture and return runaway slaves, which drew strong opposition from opponents of slavery. In 1854, a radical abolitionist, William Lloyd

Garrison, burned the Constitution because, from his perspective, it was protecting slaveholders. In 1856, Charles Sumner, senator from Massachusetts and a prominent abolitionist, was attacked and brutally beaten on the floor of the Senate by a South Carolina congressman.

Another compromise in 1854, the Kansas-Nebraska Act, changed the longstanding rules about slavery in the territories and permitted residents of Kansas Territory to vote on slavery. The result was a long and often bloody battle between free-state and slave-state supporters, a mini–civil war. Then, in 1859, John Brown, who had led a massacre of five slavery supporters in Kansas, led a group of radical abolitionists to capture the US Army's armory at Harper's Ferry in what was then western Virginia, with the goal of giving weapons to enslaved Black people so they could rebel. Brown was captured and executed, becoming a martyr to some abolitionists. This national crisis of legitimacy ended in the Civil War, or, as it was sometimes called in the North at that time, the War of the Southern Insurrection.

These national events had counterparts in San Francisco. California's constitution prohibited slavery, but some southerners brought their enslaved people to the new state. The case of Archy Lee roiled San Francisco in 1858. Lee had been born into slavery in Mississippi. In 1857, his master's son, Charles Stovall, came to Sacramento and brought Lee with him. By then, California abolitionists had become experienced in freeing enslaved people in their state. Stovall learned of this and tried to send Lee back to Mississippi. Lee asserted his freedom, ran away, and was hidden by one of Sacramento's Black families. Stovall found him and had him arrested. Several white abolitionist lawyers defended Lee, and a judge ordered him released. Stovall then went to the California Supreme Court, which ruled that, because Stovall had been ignorant of the California law prohibiting slavery, he should not be penalized by the loss of his father's slave. That court ordered Lee to return to Mississippi with Stovall.

When Stovall and Lee arrived in San Francisco to board a ship, the city's abolitionists were ready. They had Lee arrested to keep him in the state, and they accused Stovall of holding a slave illegally. San Francisco's small Black community publicized the case and sought funds throughout the state. Some of the most prominent Republican lawyers in the state represented Lee in his third court hearing. They secured a new ruling that Lee was a free man. Stovall then had Lee arrested for violating the Fugitive Slave Act, initiating a fourth trial. Crowds of whites and Blacks argued over the case on the city's streets, and sidewalk orators harangued the crowds. Lee's lawyers were successful, and Lee was set free. He soon moved to British Columbia, out of the jurisdiction of American law.

San Francisco's Crisis of Political Legitimacy

San Francisco had its own crisis of political legitimacy during the mid-1850s, when members of the city's merchant and business class took the law into their own hands, ignored the legitimately constituted authorities, and lynched a total of eight men.

The first step toward vigilantism came when San Francisco was still functioning under Mexican governmental structures. In 1849, Sam Brannan and other businessmen formed a citizens' group to suppress ruffians, especially a group known as the "Hounds." Some two hundred citizens brought a group of Hounds to trial before a special tribunal consisting of the alcalde and two special judges. The tribunal convicted nine men and, lacking a jail, banished them. This procedure did not circumvent the established authorities—the alcalde was centrally involved—but it was a step toward vigilantism as businessmen took the lead in apprehending those they considered wrongdoers. Soon after, however, the city had a full range of elected and appointed public officials to enforce laws and dispense justice.

Figure 4.3 provides data on the age and sex of the state's population in 1850. There is no separate census data for San Francisco, but San Francisco likely had a similar distribution by age and sex, perhaps with a somewhat larger proportion of women. Many males routinely armed themselves when in public. According to a reporter, more than half the members of the first session of the legislature, in 1850, "appeared in the legislative halls with revolvers and bowie knives fastened to their belts." David Terry—thirty-four years old when he became chief justice in 1857—carried both a gun and a bowie knife.

With a population made up overwhelmingly of single young men, many well-armed, it should be no surprise that the 1850s were a

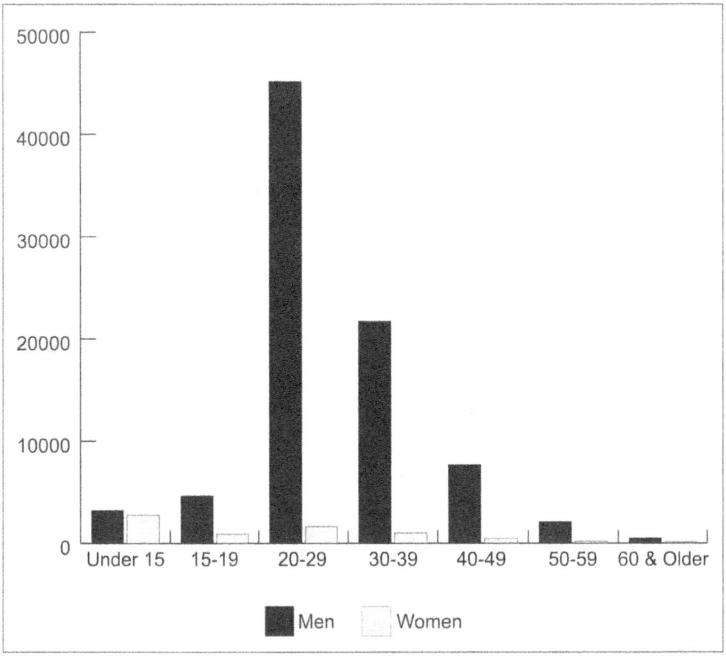

Figure 4.3. California population by sex and age at the time of the 1850 census.

violent time in the city's history. San Francisco experienced sixteen murders in 1850 and fifteen in 1851—a murder rate twelve times that of New York City.

Sydney Town was the center of San Francisco's Australian community, many of whom were thought to be former convicts, since much of Australia was a long-established British penal colony. In 1851, a series of robberies, burglaries, and arson fires were blamed on the Australians. A group of merchants and ship captains, led by Sam Brannan, formed a Committee of Vigilance. Presented with an accused burglar—an Australian, purportedly a former convict—the committee members constituted themselves as a court, convicted the accused man, and, despite rescue efforts by public officials, hanged him.

Then, claiming support from five hundred merchants and businessmen, the Committee of Vigilance seized more purported criminals, turned some of them over to the legally constituted authorities, banished others, whipped one, and hanged three more—all Australians.

The vigilantes could not imprison their victims because the jail was controlled by the legally constituted authorities, whom the vigilantes were ignoring or openly defying. The committee functioned from June to September 1851; it drew opposition from most lawyers, public officials, and political figures.

The fullest development of vigilantism came in 1856, when Charles Cora, a gambler, killed William Richardson, a US marshal. Soon after, James Casey, a member of the Board of Supervisors, shot and killed James King of William, a popular newspaper editor, who had revealed that Casey had a criminal record in New York. King had announced that he was always armed; Casey claimed self-defense.

The Committee of Vigilance was revived with William T. Coleman, a leading merchant, as president. They defied the sheriff, removed Cora and Casey from the jail, and hanged them. The committee then constituted itself as the civil authority in the city and organized a force of nearly six thousand well-armed men, drawn mostly from the city's merchants and businessmen. Their opposition included the mayor, sheriff, head of the state militia, chief justice of the state, and other prominent political figures, but they failed to maintain the rule of law. When the governor tried to reestablish the authority of the state, the vigilantes simply ignored him.

William Tecumseh Sherman, a West Point graduate, had passed through California in 1847 while serving in the war. He returned as a civilian in 1853, opened a bank, and was appointed major general of the California militia in 1856. He opposed the vigilantes but was unable to use the militia to restore the lawful authorities.

Sherman wrote to his brother: "For three months we have been governed by a self-constituted committee, who have hung four men, banished some twenty others, imprisoned, and ironed [that is, put into shackles] many men, and who now hold a judge of the [state] Supreme Court in their power, the authorities being utterly unable to do anything. . . . There is no doubt we have had a bad situation of law here, and more than a fair share of rowdies, but I think the committee itself no better . . . My own opinion is the committee is tired of its position, but finds it difficult to withdraw from the complications in which they are involved." Sherman resigned his militia commission

Figure 4.4. The vigilantes barricaded their headquarters with sandbags. They called it Fort Vigilance, but it was usually called Fort Gunnybags. Note the sentries on the roof and the bell to sound an alarm. Photo wnp37.02118, courtesy OpenSFHistory.

and left California. A few years later, during the Civil War, he emerged as the most important Union commander after Ulysses S. Grant.

The vigilantes of 1856 hanged four men and banished thirty to forty. When they tried to arrest David Terry, the chief justice of the California Supreme Court, he resisted and cut one of the vigilantes with his bowie knife. The vigilantes then put Terry on trial for murder, but, fortunately for Terry, the man recovered. As Sherman said, the vigilantes seemed not to know how to get out of the situation they had created. If they returned power to the lawful authorities, they could be charged with murder and insurrection. Instead, they held onto power, established a political party, and elected themselves to local office. This party and its successors (under various names) dominated city politics for most of the next twenty years, institutionalizing government by merchants and businessmen.

In the late nineteenth and early twentieth centuries, popular accounts of the vigilantes glorified them, treating them as saviors of the city—outraged citizens justified in taking matters into their own hands and cleansing their community. They were presented as having had no choice but to overthrow the legally constituted authorities and pass judgement on dangerous criminals. Recent historians have argued to the contrary, that action outside the law was unnecessary, that the businessmen who made up the Committee of Vigilance scarcely pursued—much less exhausted—legal courses of action. They were too preoccupied with business to bother with politics, and then they took a shortcut rather than pursuing legal remedies.

The vigilante episodes of the 1850s had a long afterlife. Some San Franciscans subsequently invoked the vigilantes during times of civic crisis that allegedly required extralegal action. San Francisco's last significant episode of vigilantism was in 1934 (see chapter 7). But later vigilantism did not include lynching.

San Francisco and the Civil War

One of the complaints of the vigilantes was that city government was dominated by a political organization headed by David Broderick, an Irish Catholic Democrat from New York City. Broderick had built a strong Democratic party organization in San Francisco using techniques he learned in New York, and he soon dominated the state legislature through his influence among the San Francisco members. He defended working people, opposed the Fugitive Slave Act, defended the rights of free Black people, and strongly opposed slavery. Broderick was elected to the US Senate in 1857, but he soon came into conflict with the state's other US senator, leader of the state's Chivalry Democrats who were aligned with the southern, proslavery wing of the national Democratic party.

In 1859, David Terry, former chief justice of the state supreme court and a leading member of the Chivalry faction, challenged Broderick to a duel. Duels were illegal but still common. Broderick's gun discharged prematurely, permitting Terry to take deadly aim. Broderick's death made him a martyr to the antislavery cause, as his supporters widely quoted his supposed dying words: "They have killed me because I was opposed to slavery and a corrupt administration."

In the 1860 presidential election, San Franciscans voted for Abraham Lincoln, Republican and opponent of slavery, giving him just under 7,000 votes, compared to 4,000 for Stephen Douglas, candidate of the northern wing of the Democratic party. The proslavery candidate of the southern wing of the Democratic party got under 2,600. Lincoln's victory prompted the secession first of South Carolina and then the rest of the South, leading to war.

In San Francisco and throughout California, supporters of the Union cause held public rallies. Union Square, now center of the downtown shopping district, got its name from the many pro-Union rallies held there. Thomas Starr King, pastor of the Unitarian church, undertook grueling speaking campaigns around the state to promote the Union cause. Inspired in part by King's oratory, Californians made their most impressive contribution to the Union in gold, especially in donations for the Sanitary Commission, a voluntary organization formed to care for wounded Union soldiers. Though only 2 percent of the Union's population, Californians donated more than a quarter of all funds raised by the Sanitary Commission. California's contributions, furthermore, were in gold, which had greater purchasing power than the depreciated greenbacks (paper money) that the Lincoln administration was issuing to help pay for the war. California gold, sent regularly to New York from San Francisco by ship, played a significant role in helping to stabilize Union finances and preventing the runaway inflation that plagued the Confederacy.

In the 1864 presidential election, Lincoln and the Republicans easily carried California. Throughout the Civil War, most Californians remained loyal to the Union, but there were exceptions. David Terry became an officer in the Confederate army, and other Californians also joined the Confederate ranks. A few Confederate sympathizers schemed to separate Southern California or to disrupt the shipment of California gold to the Union, but nothing came of such plotting. After 1863, however, there was real concern about the Confederate navy ships that were attacking US shipping in the Pacific. Army engineers

Figure 4.5. This rally on Market Street was called in support of the Union. The large banners read, "The Union, The Whole Union, and Nothing But the Union, Webster" and "Liberty and Union One and Inseparable." The former is a quotation from Daniel Webster. This may have been one of the rallies where King spoke. Photo by Carleton Watkins, *Union Mass Meeting, Market, Post and Montgomery Sts., S.F., Cal.*, negative, February 22, 1861, courtesy the J. Paul Getty Museum, Los Angeles.

had begun to build Fort Point, at the Presidio of San Francisco, in 1853 as part of a system to defend the Bay. In 1861, it was rushed to completion because of concern about protecting the gold shipments. The army also heavily fortified Alcatraz Island to defend the Bay.

San Francisco's Black community strongly supported both the Union cause and their own rights. In 1863, Charlotte Brown, a young Black woman, took a stand against racial discrimination on San Francisco's streetcars, which were then privately owned. Her father had recently started the city's first Black newspaper, *Mirror of the Times*. She was on her way to a doctor's appointment when a streetcar conductor told her "colored persons" were not allowed. She protested but was forced off the car. She sued the company. The ruling was in her favor, but the court awarded her only five cents, the amount of the streetcar fare, and allowed the streetcar company to continue its discrimination.

Racial discrimination on the city's streetcars did not end until a few years later when Mary Ellen Pleasant successfully sued one of the

MARK TWAIN REPORTS ON LIFE IN GOLD RUSH SAN FRANCISCO, 1863–67

Samuel Clemens visited San Francisco in June 1863 and returned in May 1864. A budding journalist, he had recently started writing under the name Mark Twain. He later wrote about San Francisco, "I fell into love with the most cordial and sociable city in the Union." He found a job as reporter for the *Morning Call* and was assigned to finding local news. He quickly found that scrambling to come up with a constant stream of local news was "fearful, soulless drudgery."

"We raked the town from end to end, gathering such material as we might," he recalled, and jocularly added, "if there were no fires to report, we started some." He was fired in October. Twain then tried prospecting for gold in Tuolumne County, where he wrote a story initially titled "Jim Smiley and His Jumping Frog," which was later retitled "The Celebrated Jumping Frog of Calaveras County." The story was published by a New York periodical. He returned to San Francisco with a new career. Now, instead of thinking of himself a reporter, he referred to himself as "a writer of literature of a low order, i.e., humorous." In 1867, he sailed to New York City as a correspondent for another San Francisco newspaper, the *Alta California*, ending his stay in San Francisco and providing his material for his first book, *Innocents Abroad*.

Though Twain is often credited with the observation that "the coldest winter I ever spent was one summer in San Francisco," there is no evidence that he ever said it and considerable evidence that he did not. But with a high fog blocking the sun and facing a cold wind off the ocean, shivering San Franciscans are likely to agree with the sentiment every August—which San Franciscans sometimes call Fogust.

streetcar companies. She was, at that time, the best-known and wealthiest Black woman in the city. She had helped to pay Archy Lee's legal fees and those of Charlotte Brown. In 1859, she had reputedly provided some financial support for John Brown's raid at Harper's Ferry.

Early in the Civil War, in October 1861, San Francisco was connected to the Eastern United States by a telegraph line, dramatically reducing the time it took for news to reach the city from the East. Stephen Field, chief justice of the California Supreme Court, sent one of the first messages over that telegraph line, to President Lincoln, assuring him of the loyalty of California. By the time the last Confederate troops surrendered in June 1865, plans were well under way to connect California to the East by rail, a development that helped to cement San Francisco's status as the metropolis of the West throughout the remainder of the nineteenth century.

5

Metropolis of the West

San Francisco's Gilded Age, 1865–1906

Historians use "the Gilded Age" to refer to the time in US history from the end of the Civil War to about 1900. *The Gilded Age* was the title of the first novel by onetime San Francisco resident, Mark Twain, coauthored with his Connecticut neighbor, Charles Dudley Warner, and published in 1873. In it, Twain and Warner satirized the materialism and corruption of their day. "Gilded Age" is also an appropriate term to describe San Francisco in that time period. Gilding is a process that covers inexpensive base metal with a shiny top coat. The glittering image of San Francisco during that era included rapid economic development based in significant part on new technologies in transportation and manufacturing and the emergence of a wealthy class that included many who had profited from those new technologies. They put their stamp on the city and region, including erecting the tallest buildings west of St. Louis. But the gleaming surface sometimes hid what lay underneath. Both nationally and in San Francisco, it was an age not only of great fortunes and powerful new technologies but also of grinding urban poverty and vicious racism.

Metropolis of the West

San Francisco continued to grow rapidly, continuously ranking among the ten largest cities in the country from 1870 through 1900. In 1890, it was the largest city west of St. Louis, with almost six times as many residents as Los Angeles.

James Bryce, an English lord and a perceptive journalist, traveled the United States in the 1880s collecting material for *The American Commonwealth* (1888), a book still highly useful for understanding the US at that time. Bryce said about San Francisco: "California, more than any other part of the Union, is a country by itself, and San Francisco a capital. . . . San Francisco dwarfs the other [western] cities, and is a commercial and intellectual centre, and source of influence for the surrounding regions, more powerful over them than is any Eastern city over its neighborhood."

What made San Francisco the metropolis of the West? It was the largest city, but more significantly, as Bryce indicated, its banks and corporate headquarters dominated the economic—and sometimes political—life of much of the region.

During the Gold Rush, some individuals had quickly realized that more money was to be made by selling picks and shovels than by working with them. Sam Brannan, a storekeeper in what was about to become the Gold Country, helped to set off the Gold Rush by running through the streets of San Francisco yelling about the discovery of gold. First, however, he reputedly bought up all available picks and shovels for his store. Successful Gold Country merchants parlayed small investments into considerable fortunes, then invested in other fields, including banking, railroads, manufacturing, and agriculture. They may have started with a small store in the Gold Country, but the most successful soon moved to San Francisco.

As mining developed throughout the West, it required technologically advanced equipment and reliable transportation to remote areas, both of which required large amounts of capital. In many developing economies, capital comes from investors in more established regions, and outsiders end up controlling important aspects of the economy. Given the development of well-capitalized banks in San Francisco, San Francisco investors played a prominent role in the development of California, Nevada, and other areas west of the Rockies, including Alaska and the independent kingdom of Hawaii.

Nevada was especially important, because the Gold Rush was followed by a Silver Rush. Between 1859 and 1880, a third of a billion dollars in silver (equivalent to more than $8 billion in 2025) was taken out of the Comstock Lode. Much of this came from deep-shaft mining in remote areas, requiring large amounts of capital to develop both mines and railroad lines. Stocks in mining companies were bought and sold at San Francisco's Mining Exchange, scene of quick profits and devastating losses. San Francisco was the financial center not only for the Nevada silver boom but also for mining throughout much of the intermountain West. And the profits flowed to San Francisco, helping both to develop California industries and to build lavish mansions for a few.

William Chapman Ralston was among the first to rake in extraordinary profits from the Comstock. He organized the Bank of California in 1864 and set up agencies in the Comstock region. William Sharon, Ralston's representative there, used the bank's resources to gain control of many mines. Ralston's bank used the profits to invest in manufacturing, mostly in San Francisco, including foundries and ironworks, a refinery for Hawaiian sugar, and woolen mills to make cloth from the wool of California sheep. Other investments included shipping, gold mining, insurance, agriculture, and the Palace Hotel, modeled on the great luxury hotels of Europe. In 1875, however, Ralston faced a financial crisis. He sold his share of the Palace Hotel to Sharon, disposed of other stock as best he could, resigned from the bank, and died the same day. Sharon, who was elected to the US Senate from Nevada in 1873, took over the reorganized Bank of California.

By then, the Bank of California had been displaced as the dominant factor in Nevada silver mining, losing out to four partners, James G. Fair and John W. Mackay, both experienced mine operators, and James C. Flood and William F. O'Brien, San Francisco saloonkeepers turned stockbrokers. These four—all Irish—wrested control of one large mine from Sharon in 1868, and the mine almost immediately began to produce large profits. Fair succeeded Sharon in the US Senate. The four invested their profits widely. Flood took the lead in creating the Nevada Bank of San Francisco in 1875 and served as its president. The Nevada Bank briefly claimed the largest capitalization of any bank in the country but later merged with Wells Fargo Bank.

George Hearst provides a different example. Growing up in a mining region in Missouri, he became a self-taught mining engineer. In 1859, he borrowed funds to buy a one-sixth interest in the Ophir Mine in Nevada, which proved extraordinarily profitable. He invested widely, including the Homestake Mine in South Dakota, one of the most productive gold mines in the nation; the Anaconda Mine in Montana, a copper mine that once produced one-fifth of the world's copper; and agricultural, ranching, and timber lands throughout the West. A Democrat, he bought a financially shaky newspaper, the *San Francisco Examiner*, as a service to his party and a boost to his own political career. He soon turned the newspaper over his son, William Randolph Hearst. George Hearst served in the US Senate from 1886 until his death in 1891. In the twentieth century, William Randolph Hearst created a publishing empire, with newspapers in major cities across the country.

Four Sacramento merchants who prospered in the Gold Rush—Leland Stanford, Collis Huntington, Mark Hopkins, and Charles Crocker, later known as the Big Four—invested in a railroad company, the Central Pacific, that secured a huge land grant from Congress to build tracks east from Sacramento, not coincidentally running through the silver-mining region in Nevada, and then connecting in Utah to the Union Pacific, thereby creating the first transcontinental rail line. The Big Four moved their headquarters from Sacramento to San Francisco and organized the Southern Pacific (SP) to build and operate a rail line south through California, across Arizona, New Mexico, and Texas to New Orleans, and other lines centered on the Bay Area. The SP also had fleets of ships that carried passengers and freight along the Pacific Coast, between New Orleans and New York, and between California and Japan. By the late 1880s, the SP claimed to be the largest transportation system in the nation, with more than nine thousand miles of rails and sixteen thousand miles of water lines. Until the 1890s, it had a virtual monopoly on rail traffic within the Bay Area. The SP was also the largest landowner in California until the corporation was dismantled in the 1990s. And the SP was long considered to be the most powerful influence in California politics. Huntington, especially, was a powerful political figure behind the scenes. Crocker's son, William, head of Crocker Bank, invested throughout the region and was prominent in Republican politics in the early twentieth century. Stanford served as governor from 1862 to 1863 and as US senator from 1885 to his death in 1893. In 1885, Leland and Jane Stanford founded Stanford University as a memorial to their only child, Leland Junior, who had died of typhus at the age of fifteen.

Figure 5.1. The Spreckels Building, with the offices of the *San Francisco Call*, dominates this undated postcard from about 1900. The light-colored building just left of the Spreckels Building, across Third Street, is the Hearst Building, with the offices of the *San Francisco Examiner*. Directly across the street from the Hearst building is the de Young Building, with the large clock tower, which housed the *San Francisco Chronicle*. At the time, the corner of Third and Market Streets was known as "Newspaper Corner." The de Young and Spreckels buildings still exist, but neither looks the same as in this photo. The Hearst building was badly damaged in the earthquake and fire of 1906, and a replacement was built on the same spot. The original Palace Hotel is the large, light-colored building beyond the Hearst Building; after 1906, it too was replaced with a new building on the same site. Courtesy the Miriam and Ira D. Wallach Division of Art, Prints and Photographs: Photography Collection, the New York Public Library.

Claus Spreckels was the sugar king. When the US signed a treaty with the king of Hawaii that eliminated import duties on Hawaiian sugar, Spreckels immediately went to Hawaii, made friends with the king, and acquired much of the island of Maui for a sugar plantation. His sugar refinery was in San Francisco. He added sugar beet operations in several western states and invested in ocean shipping, a railroad to compete with the Southern Pacific, and more. In 1895, Claus and his son John purchased the *San Francisco Call*, then one of the city's four daily English-language newspapers, and celebrated by moving it into a new skyscraper on Market Street, fifteen stories high and the tallest building west of Chicago.

Access to capital made San Francisco a center for manufacturing. Throughout the late nineteenth century, the largest manufacturing operations included food processing, metalworking, clothing manufacturing, and printing. Agricultural produce from the Bay Area and the Central Valley came to San Francisco for processing before being shipped to other parts of the country. In 1907, the California Fruit Cannery Association—later renamed Del Monte—built the world's largest fruit and vegetable cannery on San Francisco's northern waterfront. The area south of Market Street along the Bay included many metalworking plants, creating products for ships, railroads, and agriculture. The Union Iron Works was the largest, employing 1,200 workers in

Figure 5.2. Union Iron Works, ca. 1890. Lithograph by Bosqui Eng. & Ptg. Co., BANC PIC 1963.002:0564—D, Robert B. Honeyman, Jr. Collection of Early Californian and Western American Pictorial Material, photograph courtesy the Bancroft Library, University of California, Berkeley.

a plant spread over fifteen acres including foundries, a rolling mill, a machine shop, and a shipyard. It produced technologically advanced mining and agricultural equipment, locomotives, and ships, including US Navy vessels.

The port was central to the city's economy until the 1970s. It was the center of a coastwise trade that extended from Alaska to Mexico and was the major Pacific Coast port for cargo to and from the western

---

FRANK RONEY DESCRIBES WORKING AT UNION IRON WORKS, 1875

Frank Roney was born in Belfast in 1841, a time when England controlled all of Ireland. As an apprentice ironworker, he not only learned the skills of that craft but also gained an understanding of the dignity of labor and the importance of a strong union. Exiled for activities against the British, he came to the US and worked in several places before landing in San Francisco in 1875. He later wrote about his experience working in San Francisco.

> I . . . went to the Union Iron Works and secured a job, although I had been advised of the tyrannous reputation of Mr. Dimmick, the foreman. . . . The American style of working, which I noticed in New York, St. Louis, and Chicago, consisted of competing to secure the favor of the foreman and through that means retain steady employment. It was carried to the limit in the Union Iron Works. No foreman was needed to urge these men to work to the point of exhaustion. They labored hard of their own volition and displayed an eagerness most discouraging to one who wished to see each of them occupy the niche of a man.
>
> It looked as if my stay would be brief in such a place working among men so utterly selfish and slavish. . . . I never hurried and always suppressed any disposition that I might have had to take work away from others. . . . [However, the foreman] was a thinking man and was strongly disposed to be fair. . . . I became a steady worker in that plant.

In his memoirs, Roney also recalled that he had been "interested in the newspaper reports of attacks upon the Chinese, which I considered unreasonable and antagonistic to the principles of American Liberty." When Anton Refregier created his mural at Rincon Annex in the 1940s (see p. 106), he included Roney's comment as part of his mural depicting the anti-Chinese riots of the 1870s.

In the 1880s, Roney became a leader in efforts to form unions, but eventually returned to his craft of ironworker. He set down his reminiscences after 1910, when he could no longer work and lived with a son in Los Angeles.

---

part of the United States. The federal census of San Francisco in 1900 counted more than six thousand people working in food processing, nearly five thousand in metalworking plants, and nearly the same number in clothing and shoes factories. But some ten thousand people worked on the waterfront as longshoremen, seamen, teamsters, or ship repair and provisioning crews. Because of the port, there were also many warehouses along the waterfront.

San Francisco Expands

During the Gilded Age, as San Francisco's population grew, the city expanded dramatically. Much of the city's development at that time resulted not from any central planning but instead from decisions by many individual entrepreneurs.

The center of the city in the 1850s and early 1860s was Portsmouth Square. Ralston, in 1866, relocated his Bank of California to the corner of California and Sansome Streets. Other financial and commercial firms followed, establishing the financial district along California and Montgomery Streets. Ralston invested heavily in the South of Market area and tried to shift the emerging central business district further southward, toward his holdings. He proposed to extend Montgomery Street straight south, creating a boulevard cutting diagonally across the blocks south of Market Street. Blocked by lawsuits and political opposition, he managed only to create New Montgomery Street, merely two blocks long. In 1872, still trying to move the center of the business district southward, he chose the junction of New Montgomery and Market Streets as the site for his Palace Hotel, constructed between 1873 and 1875 and modeled on the most prominent hotels of Europe. Ralston once claimed, "what is for the good of the masses will in the end be of equal benefit to the bankers," but he usually acted on the premise that what was good for his own ventures was good for the city.

During these years, the city expanded both vertically and horizontally, based on new technologies. One new technology was the steel-frame skyscraper, which permitted the construction of such tall downtown buildings as the Spreckels Building. In the late nineteenth century, downtown San Francisco boomed with the construction of tall buildings, as the city's economic leaders sought to outdo each other with the height and grandeur of their corporate headquarters. By 1900 or so, the city had developed a well-defined central business district, with financial institutions centered along California and Montgomery Streets, and a retail shopping district along Grant and Powell Streets, anchored by the new Emporium department store on Market Street opposite Powell Street. Large luxury hotels and theaters rounded out the central business district.

The other new technology was the cable car, which accelerated the construction of residential suburbs. Previously, there had been horse-drawn streetcars, but horses could not pull cars up the city's steep hills. Andrew Hallidie, who had developed a superior variety of metal cable for use in mining, envisioned a streetcar that could be attached to a moving underground cable powered by a steam engine in a central location. The first cable-car line went into operation in 1873, and the idea spread rapidly. By 1890, there were twenty-three lines, radiating outward from the central business district to outlying residential areas and making it possible for many San Franciscans to live further from the center of the city. The upper-income and middle-income neighborhoods west of downtown were especially well-served, with lines on nearly every east-west street. Now middle-class businessmen and professionals could ride to work on cable cars from their homes in the Western Addition or Pacific Heights. Their wives and daughters could ride cable cars from their homes to the downtown retail shopping district.

The construction of the elaborate network of cable-car lines was driven by individual entrepreneurs, who applied to the Board of Supervisors—and sometimes bribed supervisors—for a franchise (a permit) to build a streetcar line on a particular street. As streetcar lines extended into parts of the city where there were no residences, development soon followed, creating streetcar suburbs. Patterns of residential construction were also set by individual builders with only minimal oversight from the city. Some 1,500 building contractors and developers were active in the city in the 1880s and 1890s. Fernando Nelson, the most prolific of these builders, put up some four thousand houses over his long career. City planning as we know it today—with building code and zoning regulations that specify the type of construction possible in any given area—was far in the future.

The Western Addition and Pacific Heights developed as middle- and upper-class streetcar suburbs, but the Mission District had a more working-class character, although there were also many middle-class and a few upper-class areas there. Streetcar lines from the Mission District carried young, mostly unmarried women to jobs downtown as typists or retail-store clerks. The same streetcar lines carried men to jobs in the manufacturing and warehouse district south of Market Street. Many who worked south of Market Street also lived there, often in crowded tenements, and walked to work. Though residents of the new streetcar suburbs might work or shop downtown, the new residential neighborhoods quickly began to develop their own identities, with grocery stores, schools, firehouses, churches and synagogues, saloons and temperance societies, and meeting halls.

Jack London, born in 1876, grew up in the South of Market working-class neighborhood. In 1909, now a successful author, he wrote: "Old San Francisco . . . was divided midway by the Slot. The Slot was an iron crack that ran along the center of Market street, and from the Slot arose the burr of the ceaseless, endless cable that was hitched at will to the cars it dragged up and down. In truth, there were two slots, but in the quick grammar of the West time was saved by calling them, and much more that they stood for, 'The Slot.'" He continued, "North of the Slot were the theaters, hotels, and shopping district, the banks and the staid, respectable business houses. South of the Slot were the factories, slums, laundries, machine-shops, boiler works, and the abodes of the working class." There's some exaggeration in London's description, because many of the things he describes as north of Market Street were also to be found south of Market, and vice versa. But, in general, London's description of a city divided by Market Street had a considerable basis in the reality.

A City of Immigrants

The 1870 census found San Francisco to have the largest proportion of immigrants of any US city. The two largest non-British immigrant groups in the US—and in San Francisco—were German and Irish.

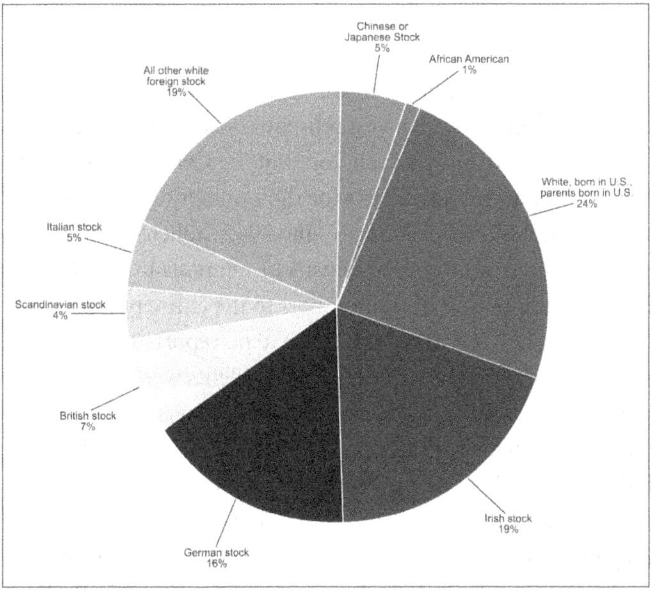

Figure 5.3. San Francisco ethnicity and race based on 1900 census data.

Midwestern cities tended to be more German than Irish. Northeastern cities tended to be more Irish than German. San Francisco and New York City were unusual as having nearly equal percentages of both groups.

The 1900 census provides the best picture of the city's ethnicity during these years. It includes data on place of birth, parents' place of birth, and language, all relevant for thinking about ethnicity. Figure 5.3 indicates that three-quarters of the city's residents were first- or second-generation immigrants, the large majority from Europe. In the chart, "stock" refers to people whose parents were born in a particular place, so it includes both immigrants and the children of immigrants. British stock includes those from Great Britain or areas settled by the British. Scandinavian stock includes those from Denmark, Norway, Sweden, and Iceland; Swedes were most numerous. German stock includes Austrians. The individual groups in "all other foreign stock" each accounted for fewer than 4 percent of the total. This is, of course, a snapshot in time, as of April 1900. In the previous decade, there had been growing numbers from Italy and other parts of southern Europe and from the Russian Empire and other parts of eastern Europe.

Race, place of origin, and language are important aspects of ethnicity. So is religion, but data on religion is less available. The US census has never asked anyone's religion, but the Census Bureau sometimes asked religious organizations for the number of their members. Different religious organizations counted their adherents differently. Converting data from the 1906 census of religious bodies to a common base and comparing those numbers to the entire population suggests that almost half the city's residents had no reported religious membership. About 40 percent of the city's residents were Catholic, about 10 percent belonged to Protestant denominations (the largest were the Congregationalists, Episcopalians, Lutherans, Methodists, and Presbyterians), and about 2 percent were Jewish.

There was no one-to-one connection between place of origin and religion. Germans were highly diverse, including Calvinists, Catholics, Lutherans, and Jews. British immigrants could be Catholic, Episcopal, Methodist, Presbyterian, or Jewish. Russians could be Orthodox, Molokan, or Jewish. Catholics could be German, French, Irish, Italian, Latino, or of another background. The northeastern part of the city, today called North Beach, was then called the Latin Quarter, home to many Italians, French people, and Latinos. Its churches, Saints Peter and Paul and St. Francis, were mostly Italian, and Our Lady of Guadalupe was mostly Spanish-speaking. Notre Dame des Victoires was French. Elsewhere in the city, Germans including German Jews tended to be more numerous in the Western Addition, and Irish were more likely to be found South of Market and in the Mission District, but none of those neighborhoods were exclusively of one ethnic group.

Ethnic bonds were important for late-nineteenth-century San Franciscans, and ethnic groups created their own institutions. Hospitals provide one example. The French Hospital was San Francisco's first private hospital, founded in 1851. St. Mary's Hospital was organized in 1857 by the Catholic Sisters of Mercy, who were predominantly Irish. In 1858, the German General Benevolent Society formed the German Hospital (now Davies). Mount Zion Hospital was established in 1887 by the Jewish community to serve anyone "needy and distressed." Ethnic groups, often religious, also organized orphanages and a variety of other beneficial societies.

A Reputation for Tolerance

Most historians agree that San Francisco and Northern California in the late nineteenth and early twentieth centuries were characterized by an unusual degree of tolerance for religious differences. Some attribute this to the Gold Rush, when everyone—that is, everyone who was white—was essentially equal in the struggle to find riches. San Franciscans elected an Irish-Catholic mayor in 1867, many years before either New York City or Boston. Adolph Sutro, who was Jewish, was elected mayor of San Francisco in 1894, nearly eighty years before New York City elected its first Jewish mayor.

San Francisco's reputation for tolerance extended to vice. Some nineteenth-century San Franciscans seemed almost to take a perverse pride in the brothels, dance halls, gin mills, and gambling dens of the Barbary Coast. Every deep-water sailor of the nineteenth century vowed to get to the city at least once to sample its storied pleasures.

The presence of such a large vice district derived in major part from the city's large population of single men. In 1890, San Francisco included 124,000 males over the age of ten, of whom 57 percent were unmarried. Some three thousand seamen called the city their home port, giving San Francisco more sailors than any other American city, even New York. The seasonal nature of employment in California agriculture, mining, and lumbering meant that as many as forty thousand men spent their winters in the cheap lodging houses and hotels near the waterfront and south of Market Street. Given the western economy that depended on large numbers of seasonal laborers and the Pacific Coast transportation that required a fleet of coastal schooners, it is almost inevitable that San Franciscans tolerated a large vice district, catering to the many single men who marched in the army of migratory laborers and sailed in the coastal navy.

Closing the Barbary Coast, as some moral reformers periodically demanded, would do more than eliminate what was seen as both a blot on the city's moral standing and a major tourist attraction. For middle-class and upper-class San Franciscans, closing the

Figure 5.4. Emperor Norton, in his dress uniform, ca. 1880 or earlier. Photograph by H. W. Bradley and William Rulofson, portrait file of The Bancroft Library, BANC PIC 1905.00002—POR: Norton, Joshua Abraham:1, courtesy of Bancroft Library, University of California, Berkeley.

Barbary Coast might divert thousands of rowdy sailors, lumberjacks, and miners into the places of entertainment frequented by the city's more genteel residents. Consequently, occasional efforts to close down the Barbary Coast received little support from either the city's voters or its elected officials until a state law brought the closing of the brothels in 1917.

The city also had a reputation for tolerating eccentricity. Samuel Walker, writing in *Scribner's Monthly* in 1875, claimed that "San Francisco has rather more than her share of eccentric characters." Gilded Age San Francisco not only tolerated its eccentrics—it seemed to delight in them. "Emperor" Norton was the best known. Once a successful merchant, Joshua Norton suffered reverses and apparently lost his mental stability along with his bank account. He proclaimed himself "Norton I, Emperor of North America and Protector of Mexico." For years San Franciscans indulged this fantasy, provided him with an extravagant uniform, addressed him as "Emperor Norton," and kept him in pocket money and necessities.

Norton may have inspired others, including Frederick Coombs, who dressed in colonial garb and a powered wig and walked about the streets with a banner identifying himself as "Washington the Second." Abe Warner presided over the Cobweb Palace, a waterfront saloon famous for the dusty spider webs that shrouded much of the interior. And there were others.

The Limits of Tolerance

Such oddities may have contributed to the city's reputation for tolerance, but San Franciscans were clearly more tolerant of a handful of bizarre individuals than of large numbers of people of a different race. The claim that *all* were equal during the Gold Rush was never accurate. It would be more accurate to say that all European-origin whites were essentially equal. A Foreign Miners Tax was actually aimed at Chinese and Latino miners. From the start of Chinese immigration to California, some viewed them as a threat and portrayed them as unclean, immoral, clannish, and heathen. "Coolie" was a derogatory term for a Chinese laborer, and "anti-coolie" clubs attracted members in working-class neighborhoods of San Francisco. State and city laws discriminated against the Chinese from the 1850s onward. In San Francisco, the Chinese were largely segregated in Chinatown. Venturing outside Chinatown could be dangerous, as they were sometimes beaten.

Depression, the Workingmen's Party, and After

Race and class came together in San Francisco in the 1870s. Nationwide, the late 1870s were years of economic depression and high unemployment. In July 1877, a strike by Eastern railroad workers, protesting wage cuts, mushroomed into violence in Midwestern and Eastern cities. In San Francisco, a rally to support the strikers erupted into a riot aimed at Chinese workers.

That fall, Denis Kearney attracted many white working-class followers when he condemned the monopoly power of the SP and, at the same time, argued that monopolists were using Chinese workers to drive down wages for white workers. Kearney formed the Workingmen's Party of California (WPC) with the slogan "The Chinese Must Go." His intemperate attacks on the Chinese and the city's economic elite brought both official and vigilante responses. The mayor directed the police to break up public meetings of the WPC, and Kearney and other party leaders were repeatedly arrested. In a resurgence of vigilantism, William T. Coleman, head of the 1856 Committee of Vigilance, formed a Committee of Safety, a group armed with pick handles and quickly labeled the "Pick Handle Brigade." Nonetheless, the WPC dominated political life in San Francisco in the late 1870s, sweeping elections in 1878 and 1879.

In 1882, this anti-Chinese prejudice reached the US Congress. Senator John Miller, a California Republican who began his political career in San Francisco, introduced a bill to exclude Chinese immigration for ten years and to extend a previous ban on Chinese becoming naturalized citizens. Miller's bill passed by large margins; the Chinese Exclusion Act prohibited entry to all Chinese except teachers, students, merchants, tourists, and officials. It was renewed and extended in 1892 and made permanent in 1902.

Another consequence of the events of the 1870s was a surge in organization among white workers after the economy revived in the 1880s. The first recorded union activity in San Francisco came in 1849, when carpenters went on strike for higher wages. Local unions were common in the city thereafter, but most were short-lived until the 1880s when Frank Roney, among others, led organizing drives. In the 1880s, many local unions affiliated with newly formed national unions and sometimes with the American Federation of Labor (AFL), which was organized in 1886. Such unions typically limited their membership to skilled workers in a particular field, such as carpentry or printing, and many excluded women and people of color. California's unions in the 1880s often presented themselves as defending white workers against competition from Chinese workers, arguing that employers used Chinese workers to drive down wage levels and working conditions. Most historians agree that opposition to Chinese labor gave California unions what the historian Alexander Saxton called "the indispensable enemy."

Henry George, a San Francisco journalist in the 1870s, witnessed the political upheaval of the Workingman's Party. In his *Progress and Poverty* (1879), George drew upon that experience to argue that "progress" (economic growth and development) inevitably brought greater poverty, which he attributed to land speculation and monopolization. His proposed solution was a single tax on the increase in the value of land, intended to create a tax burden on large landholders that would force them to break up their holdings. *Progress and Poverty* quickly sold three million copies nationwide, and the Single-Tax became a popular panacea for the economic dislocations that afflicted many Americans in the late nineteenth century.

Chinese San Franciscans: Discrimination and Resistance

San Francisco's Chinese community encountered segregation similar to that imposed on Black people in the South, including residential and occupational segregation resulting from local custom rather than law. When segregation or discrimination was written into law, it could be challenged. In 1871 the San Francisco school board barred all Chinese students from the public schools, and the ban lasted until 1885, when the parents of Mamie Tape sued the city in *Tape v. Hurley*, forcing the city to open a segregated Chinese school. Similarly, when the San Francisco Board of Supervisors passed restrictions on Chinese laundry owners, the laundrymen hired three of the best attorneys in the city. In *Yick Wo v. Hopkins* (1886), the US Supreme Court for the first time declared a licensing law unconstitutional because local authorities used it to discriminate on the basis of race.

Figure 5.5.
The Tape family: Joseph, Emily, Mamie, Frank, and Mary, ca. 1884–85. Photographer unknown, photo courtesy the National Museum of American History.

The Chinese Exclusion Act of 1882 was followed by attacks on Chinese people in many western communities. In response, many retreated to the agricultural areas of Central California and the larger Chinatowns, especially San Francisco's. As a result, San Francisco's Chinatown actually grew in the years following the Exclusion Act. However, that was only temporary. Declining numbers of Chinese San Franciscans after 1890 reflect a return to China by some, the exclusion of new immigrants after 1882, and the impossibility of a community that was 90 percent male to maintain its numbers except through immigration. Still, by 1900, an American-born generation was beginning to come into its own in Chinatown.

SAN FRANCISCANS APPEAL TO THE US SUPREME COURT: YICK WO (1886) AND WONG KIM ARK (1898)

The man who has gone down in history as Yick Wo was actually named Lee Yick. He was born in China and came to San Francisco in 1861. He soon established a small laundry, like many others among the city's Chinese immigrants. Yick complied with all city regulations, including fire and public health rules. However, in 1880, the San Francisco Board of Supervisors required a permit for any laundry in a wooden building. Of some two hundred Chinese laundry owners in the city who requested permits, only one received a permit; of some eighty non-Chinese laundry owners, only one was denied a permit. When Yick was denied a permit, he continued to operate his laundry and subsequently was arrested, fined, and then imprisoned for refusing to pay the fine.

Yick and some 150 other Chinese laundry owners belonged to a Chinese laundry owners guild, and they challenged the permit law. To represent them in court, they hired Matthew Hall McAllister, one of the most prominent lawyers in the city and a former federal judge. On behalf of Yick, McAllister sued San Francisco sheriff Peter Hopkins, arguing that the discriminatory enforcement of the law violated the Fourteenth Amendment. The California Supreme Court and US Circuit Court ruled against Yick, so McAllister appealed to the US Supreme Court.

The Supreme Court ruled that the unequal application of the law was discriminatory and therefore violated the equal protection clause of the Fourteenth Amendment. The decision in *Yick Wo v. Hopkins* (1886) set an important precedent: "The Fourteenth Amendment to the Constitution is not confined to the protection of citizens"; it applies "to all persons . . . without regard to any differences of race, of color, or of nationality."

Today, a statue of McAllister stands on the north side of San Francisco City Hall, facing McAllister Street. And Yick Wo Elementary School serves the neighborhoods of Chinatown, North Beach, and Russian Hill.

The decision in *Yick Wo* was later cited as a key precedent for the US Supreme Court's decision in *U.S. v. Wong Kim Ark* (1898). Wong was born in San Francisco in 1873 to immigrant parents from China, who were not eligible for US citizenship under the law at that time. In 1889, he and he parents returned to China. Wong married there, returned to San Francisco to work, and went back to China in 1894. Upon returning to San Francisco in 1895, he was denied entry on the basis that he was not a citizen. With financial assistance from the Chinese Consolidated Benevolent Association, Wong went to court establish that he was a citizen. The case eventually reached the US Supreme Court.

In 1898, the US Supreme Court ruled that Wong was a citizen under the Fourteenth Amendment, which states, "All persons born or naturalized in the United States, and subject to the jurisdiction thereof, are citizens of the United States." Wong's case clearly established that all persons born in the US are citizens, regardless of the citizenship of their parents unless their parents were diplomats representing another nation.

Gilded Age San Francisco Celebrates

During the last quarter of the nineteenth century, cities and nations presented extravagant expositions as a way of attracting attention to themselves. The first such in the US was in Philadelphia in 1876, celebrating the centennial of US independence. In 1893, Chicago hosted a spectacular celebration of the four-hundredth anniversary of Columbus's arrival in the New World. San Francisco hosted such events in 1894, 1915, and 1939–40.

In 1893, Michael H. de Young, publisher of the *San Francisco Chronicle*, was impressed by the Chicago exposition and by the way it drew tourists to Chicago. In the summer of 1893, while the Chicago exposition was booming, de Young proposed that San Francisco host a midwinter fair in early 1894, as a way to draw attention both to the city's mild climate and to the city itself. By mid-1893, the national economy was crashing into a serious economic depression, and San Francisco's civic leaders saw an exposition as a way to attract tourist dollars. De Young succeeded in raising both enthusiasm and funds, and, just six months later, in late January 1894, the California Midwinter International Exposition opened. By the time it closed on July 4, it had attracted more than a million—some sources say two million—visitors.

The exposition was centered on what is now the Music Concourse in Golden Gate Park. Four large buildings around a central court housed exhibits on fine arts, agriculture and horticulture, manufactures, liberal arts, and mechanical arts, including a generator for the new technology of electric lighting throughout the exposition. Around the main buildings were amusement rides and a wild animal show. Following the lead of other expositions, there were also several racialized exhibits of people purportedly from other cultures, including an African village, a Japanese village, an Eskimo village, what was termed an Oriental village (Middle Eastern, featuring scantily clad belly dancers), and a Hawaiian village, all of which presented the inhabitants as primitive and/or exotic.

Intended to showcase San Francisco and California more generally, the exposition seems to have attracted relatively little attention outside California and neighboring areas. Nonetheless, in celebrating art, technology, and manufactures, the exposition presented the gleaming surface of San Francisco's Gilded Age, just as other aspects of the exposition showed the racism and patriarchal gender relations that underlay those accomplishments.

San Francisco and the US Empire in the Pacific

Some of the exhibits at the midwinter fair had emphasized the city's links to eastern Asia and Hawaii, which, by then, was no longer a kingdom. In 1893, group of white sugar growers had overthrown Queen Liliuokalani, declared a republic, and asked to be annexed to the US. When President Grover Cleveland learned that US Marines had a role in overthrowing the monarchy, he refused the request for annexation, but the issue persisted and played a minor role in the 1896 presidential election.

In 1898, the US went to war with Spain. The war was short, and the US acquired a colonial empire: the Philippine Islands, Puerto Rico, and Guam. During the war, the US annexed Hawaii. Soon after, in 1899, by treaty with Britain and Germany, the US acquired the eastern Samoan Islands in the South Pacific. Almost overnight, the US had become a major colonial power. Not all the residents of its new acquisitions welcomed that change. A war soon broke out in the Philippines between US troops and Filipinos seeking independence.

By then, the Presidio of San Francisco had become a major US military post, charged with defending the Bay against any foreign power. In 1885, US authorities identified San Francisco as the second most important US harbor, and work was underway to strengthen fortifications around the entrance to the Bay. After the Civil War, the Presidio served as one of the most important army posts on the Pacific Coast, and troops stationed there took part in military operations against Indigenous peoples who refused to accept the reservations to which they had been assigned, notably the Modoc War of 1872–73, the Nez Perce campaign of 1877, and the campaign against Geronimo's Apaches in 1885–86. The surrender of Geronimo brought a change to the army in the western US, as many small forts were closed and troops were transferred to larger bases including the Presidio. The Presidio's iconic Montgomery Street barracks were constructed between 1895 and 1897.

Figure 5.6. The Montgomery Street Barracks were constructed as housing for enlisted men during the expansion of the Presidio in the 1890s. This photo was probably taken about 1898, shortly after the construction was complete. From TASC Negative Collection, GOGA 35031. Courtesy Golden Gate National Recreation Area, Park Archives.

Figure 5.7. Soldiers of Company H, 24th Infantry, in Yosemite National Park in 1899. At that time, the army was segregated; the 24th Infantry was one of several Black units. Courtesy Yosemite Park Archives, National Park Service.

A new role for the cavalry began in 1886, when a cavalry troop was sent to Yellowstone National Park, the nation's first national park, beginning thirty years of park administration by the army. In the fall of 1890 the federal government established three national parks in California—Yosemite, Sequoia, and General Grant—and the army undertook to manage and protect these new parks. From 1890 to 1913, army units rotated through the Presidio and the three national parks, spending the winter at the Presidio and the summer in the parks. This duty was sometimes assigned to units returning from the Philippines, perhaps as a reward for their service there in the war against Filipinos seeking independence.

With the US acquisition of possessions in the Pacific and the outbreak of war in the Philippines, the Presidio acquired another new role. Most of the war in the Philippines was over within three years, but scattered resistance to US authority continued for another ten years or so. During and after the war, the Presidio was the major assembly point for US Army forces going to the Philippines and also managed logistics and supply for the troops there. It remained central to the training and supply chain for US troops in the Pacific for much of the twentieth century.

San Francisco's Gilded Age symbolically ended with a jolt in 1906. The city's Progressive Era, however, had already begun.

6

San Francisco's Progressive Era, 1890–1919

Historians refer to the years from about 1890 until US involvement in World War I (1917–18) as the Progressive Era. At the national level, Presidents Theodore Roosevelt (1901–9) and Woodrow Wilson (1913–21) called for new laws to regulate railroads, break up monopolies, and regulate banking. A wide range of other reforms were also in the air, from federal ownership of railroads and municipal ownership of public utilities to woman suffrage and the prohibition of alcoholic beverages. San Francisco had its own Progressive Era, producing changes that have persisted to the present.

Gender, Class, and Reform in the 1890s

By 1890, the distribution of San Francisco's population by age and sex looked more like that of the rest of the nation, although men still outnumbered women for the ages between about twenty and sixty. In part this represents the port, because many of the men who worked as seafarers were unmarried, lived in the city only between voyages, but kept a San Francisco boardinghouse as their permanent address. However, census counts in April missed many single men who were seasonal workers in agriculture, lumbering, and mining, and who lived in lodging houses south of Market Street during the winter months.

The 1890 and 1900 censuses found that slightly more than one-fifth of San Francisco women over the age of ten were working for wages, nearly half as domestic servants. Other women worked in manufacturing, especially food processing and making clothing, and others as sales clerks in the new department stores, or typists and bookkeepers.

Of women in professional fields, 80 percent were teachers, but there were also 176 physicians and 14 lawyers.

The fourteen female lawyers owed their livelihood to Laura de Force Gordon and Clara Shortridge Foltz, who persuaded the legislature in 1878 to allow women to practice law in the state; they also convinced the state constitutional convention in 1879 to write into the new constitution a provision protecting women's right to engage in any "lawful business, avocation, or profession." They also tried, unsuccessfully, to get the word "male" deleted from voting requirements.

Upper-class women expected—and were expected by their society—not to work for wages but instead to manage their own households, including one or more servants. They were also expected to participate in activities outside the home, especially church or synagogue, and often women's clubs. The Century Club, founded in 1888, had the vision of uniting professional and upper-class women to serve as leaders in community betterment. Such clubs often undertook programs to assist those considered "less fortunate."

Phoebe Apperson Hearst, wife of George Hearst, was the first president of the Century Club and participated in other clubs. She and Jane Stanford, wife of Leland Stanford, were leaders in creating free kindergartens—childcare centers for working mothers. (Public schools did not offer kindergarten until much later.) Hearst also contributed funds for an orphanage, a medical school for women, and a settlement house, which provided social services for the poor. A early biographer reported that she "has an insatiable desire to help girls get an education." A central figure in supporting the University of California, she endowed its first scholarships for women, contributed funds for buildings, and, in 1897, was appointed to the Board of Regents, one of the most significant public offices held by an American woman at that time. Hearst exemplified many expectations of her day about upper-class women's social roles even as she challenged some constraints on women's involvement beyond the home and the family. She worked with Jane Stanford on some of these projects. They were in Washington, DC, at the same time when their husbands were US senators, and they became widows at about the same time. As a widow, Stanford directed much of the development of Stanford University, insisting that women

PHOEBE APPERSON HEARST ENDORSES WOMAN SUFFRAGE, 1911

Phoebe Apperson Hearst was born in a rural area in Missouri in 1842. As a girl, she had few opportunities for education. After marrying George Hearst, her husband's wealth made it possible for her to pursue her own education and to work tirelessly to improve the welfare of women and children, especially through education.

In 1896, when Californians first voted on woman suffrage, Hearst quietly donated $1,000 (equivalent to more than $38,000 in 2025) to the campaign. It was the largest single contribution, but she declined to make a public statement. She explained in a letter, "I feel that the day when women will vote is sure to come, but I have always held myself apart from the organizations that were working for suffrage because the methods did not appeal to me." She already had significant political influence and may have been unwilling to threaten that status.

By 1911, when Californians again voted on extending the suffrage to women, the national leadership of the suffrage movement had become more moderate, and Hearst concluded that she should go public with her support. Five days before the election, she announced her support at a large public rally. Newspapers headlined her announcement. In a letter to a friend, she explained her reasons: "Women should have the right to vote. I felt convinced that women would unite in favoring certain work tending towards the betterment of conditions affecting women and children particularly, which men heretofore could never be relied upon to favor when it came to the test of the ballot."

Like other advocates for woman suffrage, Hearst based her support on the need for women to participate fully in politics to protect and enhance the conditions of women and children.

In 1911, California became the sixth state to adopt woman suffrage, nine years before the Nineteenth Amendment to the US Constitution.

should be admitted and that all courses and majors be open to women, although she changed her mind about that near the end of her life.

Jane Stanford and Phoebe Apperson Hearst were unusual among upper-class women in that both supported woman suffrage, although not openly at first. In 1896, when California voters (all males) had to decide whether to amend the state constitution to enfranchise women, Stanford provided funds and free passes on the SP for suffrage organizers. The 1896 campaign for woman suffrage failed largely because of the very large negative vote in San Francisco. Those opposed to woman suffrage linked that issue with prohibition of alcohol, arguing that, if women could vote, they would approve prohibition. When California men again voted on woman suffrage in 1911, the suffrage cause benefited significantly from the advocacy of women unionists in San Francisco, who persuaded the San Francisco Labor Council to support suffrage—and it passed.

James D. Phelan and Municipal Reform

James Duval Phelan was a leader in reform efforts in the 1890s and early twentieth century. Son of a successful Gold Rush banker, Phelan inherited wealth and privilege, but, unlike most of his class, he plunged directly into city politics. Throughout the 1880s, Christopher Augustine Buckley, a saloonkeeper called the "Blind Boss" because of his impaired vision, led a Democratic party organization that dominated city politics. Phelan was among a group of young businessmen and professionals who deposed Buckley in 1890. In 1892, Adolph Sutro was elected mayor as a Populist, campaigning against the political and economic power of the Southern Pacific. (The Populists—the People's Party—favored democratic reforms, greater regulation of business, and federal ownership of railroads.)

Elected mayor in 1896, Phelan led the way to a new city charter that was designed to prevent political machines like that of Buckley. It strengthened the mayor's powers, made election of the Board of Supervisors citywide, and established the initiative and referendum. Phelan worked to improve the city's infrastructure by promoting bond issues for a new sewer system, city hospital, parks, and schools.

Phelan opposed the nineteenth-century practice of granting franchises to private corporations to provide gas, electricity, telephone, and streetcar services, arguing that such franchises created an inevitable conflict between corporations' need to make a profit and the public's need to receive service efficiently and at the lowest cost. Over previous decades, such companies' efforts to secure or protect franchises had repeatedly corrupted city politics. For Phelan, the answer was obvious: the city should own its public utilities. Toward that end, one provision in the new charter stated that the "purpose and intention of the people" was that the city's "public utilities shall be gradually acquired and owned by the City and County."

The 1901 Strike, the Union Labor Party, and the Growth of Unions

During the late nineteenth and early twentieth centuries, labor unions often developed and grew in times of economic expansion when employers needed labor and could afford to increase wages, but unions usually declined and often fell apart during "hard times," periods of economic contraction including unemployment. In San Francisco, unions grew in the prosperous 1880s, but most collapsed when employers launched an anti-union drive during the depression of the mid-1890s. Only in the late 1890s did unions begin to revive as the economy turned around.

The city's port workers organized into several unions, one for each trade. In 1901, those unions formed the City Front (that is, the waterfront) Federation, to support each other. Soon after, the recently organized Teamsters Union engaged in a life-or-death struggle with the Employers' Association, a secretive group opposed to unions. The City Front Federation voted to strike in support of the Teamsters, shutting down the port. The long, violent strike ended only through the intervention of a pro-union Catholic priest, Peter Yorke, and Governor Henry Gage. Unions continued to grow in the early twentieth century. The San Francisco Building Trades Council, consisting of unions involved in construction, was especially powerful.

Many union members concluded that the 1901 strike had lasted so long because city government aided the employers and especially because city police protected strikebreakers. Angry unionists created the Union Labor Party (ULP) to seek control of City Hall and prevent future strikebreaking by police. Andrew Furuseth of the Sailors' Union of the Pacific observed, "inasmuch as we are to have a class government, I most emphatically prefer a working class government." The new party was much like the Labour Parties then coming into existence in Britain and Australia.

In 1901, the ULP elected Eugene Schmitz, from the Musicians' Union, as mayor and reelected him in 1903 and 1905, along with other city officials. Police stopped protecting strikebreakers. In the expanding economy, unions continued to grow. In 1904, a national reporter described San Francisco as a city "where unionism holds undisputed sway." Then, in 1907, a bribery scandal brought the resignation of Schmitz and most of the supervisors, but the ULP returned to City Hall with the election of Patrick H. McCarthy, head of the Building Trades Council, as mayor in 1909.

Earthquake and Fire

At 5:12 a.m. on April 18, 1906, Californians around San Francisco Bay and for many miles north and south were jolted awake when a monstrous earthquake on the San Andreas Fault ripped along a 296-mile path centered in the ocean off the southwest corner of San Francisco. Geologists now estimate the magnitude of the earthquake as between 7.7 and 7.9. "I could see it actually coming," a San Francisco policeman said. "The whole street was undulating. It was as if the waves of the ocean were coming toward me." The earthquake twisted city streets and streetcar tracks, and broke water lines, gas pipes, and electrical power wires.

Figure 6.1. Cable-car tracks on Union Street in the aftermath of the earthquake. Photo NAID 2127302, courtesy the National Archives and Record Center.

The "new" City Hall, under construction from 1870 to 1897, collapsed. One person later suggested it had been constructed largely of "thinly varnished graft." In San Francisco's central business district, however, the new steel-frame high-rise buildings held up quite well, as did most other buildings. Some wood-frame residential buildings were knocked off their foundations, and some masonry buildings lost a wall, especially in areas where streams, marshes, or the Bay had been filled. Fires broke out almost immediately, fed by gas from broken gas pipes. Broken water mains rendered many fire hydrants useless. For three days, firefighters struggled to contain what became a firestorm—a fire of such intensity that it creates and sustains its own wind system.

General Frederick Funston, acting commander of the Presidio, sent soldiers into the city to keep order and help fight the fires. Without water, firefighters and federal troops tried to build firebreaks by demolishing buildings with dynamite. Earthquake, fire, and dynamite destroyed the heart of the city, comprising 4.11 square miles and 28,188 buildings. Of the city's 400,000 residents, some 225,000 lost their homes. Destruction was almost universal within the fire zone—corporate headquarters and tenement homes of the poor, churches and brothels. Although the official record listed 498 deaths in San Francisco, a careful search of records in the 1980s concluded that the death toll actually reached at least three thousand. Total damage, in 1906 dollars, was estimated at $400 million (equivalent to more than $14 billion in 2025), of which one-fifth was due directly to the earthquake.

Financial help poured in from individuals, organizations, and governments, including foreign governments, some $9 million in all (equivalent to about $310 million in 2024), which provided meals and temporary housing for the homeless and assistance to reestablish homes and businesses. Mayor Schmitz, under suspicion due to allegations of corruption, appointed a special committee of fifty prominent citizens, led by Phelan, to distribute the funds and plan relief and recovery. The army provided tents, field kitchens, and field hospitals for twenty refugee camps.

San Franciscans rushed to rebuild. For the city's economic and civic leaders, there was a special urgency—they feared that any delay in reconstruction would endanger their place as economic hub of the

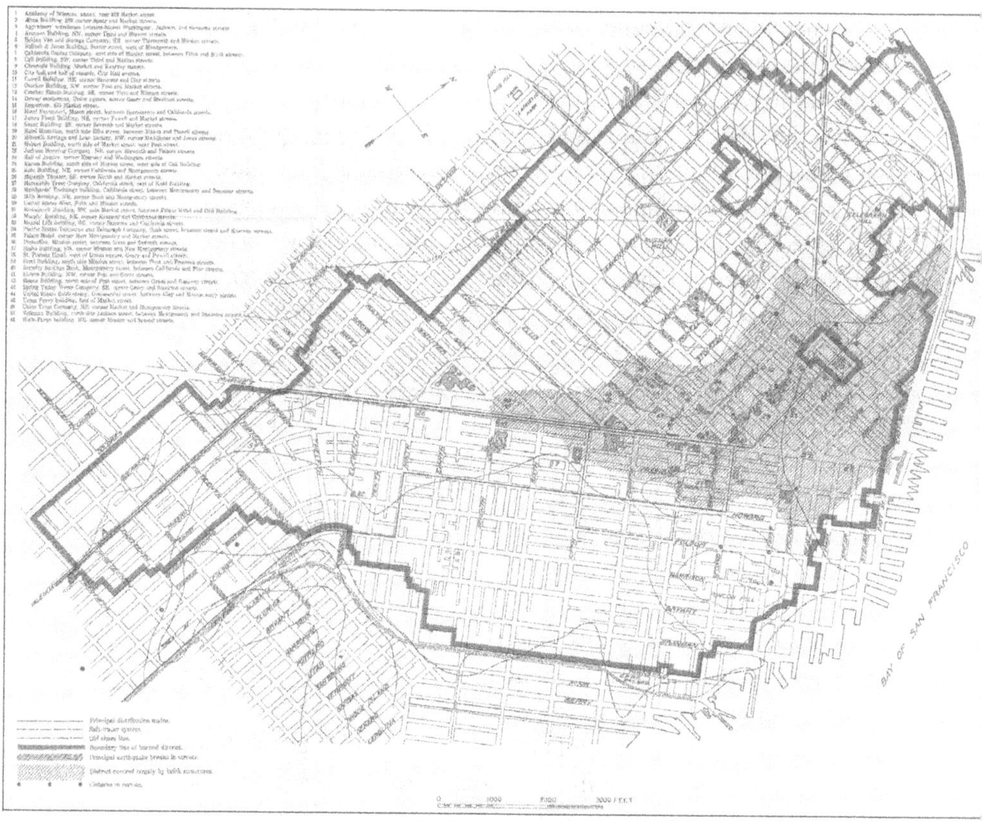

Map 6.1. This map shows the extent of the damage from the fire. The outline is of the area where destruction was near total. The shaded area is the part of the city where wooden buildings had been banned from the 1850s onward. R. L. Humphrey, *The San Francisco Earthquake and Fire of April 18, 1906*, U. S. Geological Survey, 1907, courtesy Geographicus Rare Antique Maps on Wikimedia Commons.

West. The central business district was quickly re-created in much the same location as before. In some burned residential areas near the central business district, two- and three-story wooden residences were replaced by high-rise, steel-frame buildings, creating an apartment district west of the central business district and a commercial and industrial district along major thoroughfares south of Market Street. Some civic leaders tried to use the devastation as an excuse to remove Chinatown from its location near the central business district, but they failed.

Governor George Pardee created a special commission to study the disaster. Geologists and others who studied earthquakes gained new understandings of their cause and effect. Careful examination of the effect of the earthquake on buildings helped architects and engineers to improve technologies for resisting seismic stress, and rebuilding included efforts to strengthen buildings against future earthquakes. A new, auxiliary, high-pressure water system for fighting fires was installed throughout the burned district and later extended elsewhere, including special hydrants, reservoirs, and cisterns, and water mains designed to withstand an earthquake.

Before the earthquake, in 1904, Reuben Hale, a department store owner, and an association of merchants had proposed that San Francisco should host a major international exposition to celebrate the opening of the Panama Canal. Despite the devastation of 1906, Hale and his associates did not abandon that idea. At the same time they were rebuilding downtown, they created the Panama Pacific Exposition Company and launched fundraising and lobbying efforts. In 1910, voters approved city and state bond issues for the exposition. There was strong competition for designation as the official exposition to celebrate the opening of the canal, but, in 1911, President William Howard Taft signed a congressional resolution designating San Francisco as the official site for the exposition. At a subsequent ground-breaking ceremony, President Taft called San Francisco "the city that knows how."

Rolph, Reform, and Rebuilding

By then, the city, state, and nation were in the midst of a wave of progressive reforms. President Theodore Roosevelt had launched several such programs soon after taking office in late 1901. Some states had elected progressive governors beginning in 1900, but California did not fully embrace progressivism until the administration of Governor Hiram Johnson (1911–17). Once progressivism came to state government, it produced a raft of new legislation intended to regulate many aspects of the state's economy. The state constitution was amended to include the initiative, referendum, and recall. California women gained the vote in through a constitutional amendment in 1911.

After the earthquake and fire, city government had bogged down in 1907 with the graft prosecution of Schmitz and others, and then a caretaker administration in City Hall. In 1910, under Mayor McCarthy, the city finally hired architects to design a temporary city hall. One of the progressive changes in the state constitution made all city and county elections nonpartisan. In San Francisco's first nonpartisan election, in 1911, James Rolph Jr., a popular shipowner and builder who employed only union labor, defeated McCarthy for mayor, and Rolph repeatedly won reelection until he became governor in 1931. Rolph's early years as mayor epitomized several aspects of progressivism: he embraced nonpartisanship, sought efficiency in city government, valued and relied on the advice of experts, promoted public ownership of the streetcar and water systems, and created the first city planning department.

Rolph's first years in office were a whirlwind of activity. In his inaugural address, Rolph proclaimed, "three important measures appealing to immediate attention are: A new City Hall, a public water system [and] improved street car transportation." In March 1912, the city voted on a bond issue to build a city hall and begin the Civic Center. Rolph spearheaded the campaign, worked to transfer his own popularity to the bond issue, and tied the bond issue to the Panama-Pacific International Exposition (PPIE). The bond issue carried by an eleven-to-one margin.

Plans for the Civic Center were soon complete. A new city hall was to occupy two city blocks and face an open plaza on its east. A library and an opera house were to face City Hall across the plaza. An auditorium was to stand on the south side of the plaza and a state office building on the north side.

The PPIE directors paid for the auditorium so it could be used in conjunction with the PPIE. It was completed first, in January 1915. City Hall was next, completed late in 1915. The new city hall was impressively big—Rolph delighted in telling visitors that the dome was higher than that of the national capitol—and it exuded a sense of imperial grandeur. A donation from Andrew Carnegie funded construction

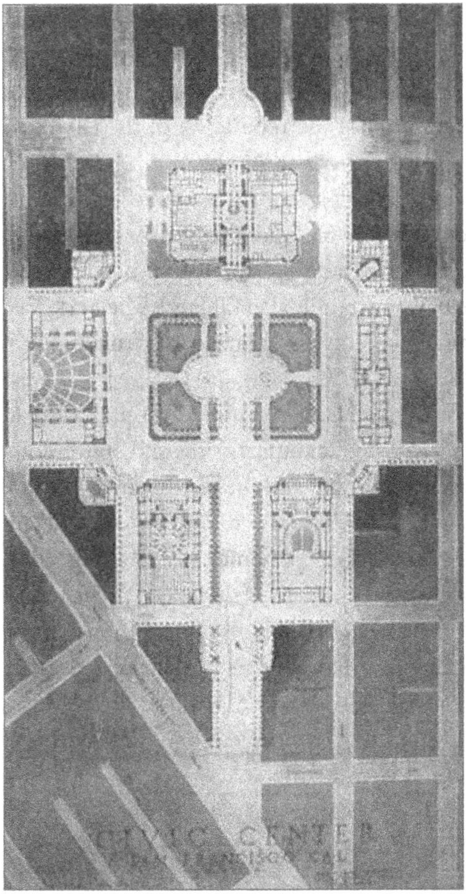

Figure 6.2. This is John Galen Howard's 1912 plan for the Civic Center. The City Hall (the large structure at the top) and the Civic Auditorium (the large structure on the left) were built first. Then came the main public library, in the lower right. An opera house (indicated at the lower left) was built much later and in a different location. The state office building (center right) was also built later. Market Street is the diagonal on the lower left. Plan of Civic Center, San Francisco, *History of the City Hall and Civic Center* by T. B. McGinnis, BANC PIC 1995.006:004A—ALB, courtesy of The Bancroft Library, University of California, Berkeley.

of the main library in early 1917. The state opened a design competition for a state office building in 1916, but war and other problems intervened, and construction was not completed until 1926. As completed, the San Francisco Civic Center embodied many of the central characteristics of the City Beautiful movement of the previous few decades: dignity, unity, harmony, and order on a monumental scale designed to inspire feelings of respect and reverence.

The PPIE was officially a celebration of the completion of the Panama Canal, but its very name, Panama-Pacific, also referred to the extension of US power in the Pacific, expressing the goals of San Francisco's civic leadership that the city be considered as both the western end of the Panama Canal, linking the Pacific Coast to the Atlantic, and also the major US port for access to the Pacific and East Asia. The PPIE was also a grand celebration of the rebuilding of the city over the previous nine years.

PPIE directors chose a location on the north side of the city, now the Marina District. Much of it was fill land, previously considered too marshy for building. The army allowed the use of much of the Presidio's frontage on the Bay, much of it also fill land. The PPIE was a great success, drawing nearly nineteen million visitors from around the country and the world.

Typical of similar expositions, the PPIE centered on palaces that presented exhibits of art, agriculture, manufacturing, transportation, and new technologies. Twenty-six states and the territories of Hawaii and the Philippines had their own exhibits, as did thirty-one foreign nations. A large "Joy Zone" provided amusements, including rides and a variety of "living exhibits" of animals, including ostriches, alligators, and manatees, and also racialized exhibits of people, including Indigenous Americans, Samoans, Maoris, Somalis, Japanese people, Chinese people, and Egyptians. Like the other expositions of the time, the exhibits of people emphasized their primitive or exotic natures, and several featured scantily clad women.

Figure 6.3. The Palace of Fine Arts, 1919. Photo by James David Givens, courtesy of Library of Congress Prints and Photographs Division.

The Palace of Fine Arts, designed by Bernard Maybeck, was so popular that it was not immediately demolished. Although designed to be temporary, it survived until the 1950s. It was completely rebuilt in the 1960s and 1970s.

Rolph had promised a first-class exposition, and the PPIE fulfilled that promise. He had promised a new city hall and had delivered in a most convincing fashion. Before the end of his first term, he had dedicated both the auditorium and the city hall and had broken ground for the new main library.

Michael M. O'Shaughnessy and New Civic Infrastructure

After Phelan left the mayor's office, he continued his efforts to bring about municipal ownership of the city's public utilities. In 1901, as a private citizen, he applied to use the Hetch Hetchy Valley as a reservoir to prevent it from falling into the hands of speculators, then transferred his claim to the city. He continually advocated that the city should directly sell San Francisco citizens not only water (by damming Hetch Hetchy and buying out the privately owned Spring Valley Water Company) but also electrical power (by generating power at Hetch Hetchy and buying out the holdings of power companies within the city).

Rolph also embraced the notion of public ownership of streetcars, water, and electricity. After the earthquake, most cable-car lines were converted to electric streetcars, but were still under private ownership. Rolph appointed Michael M. O'Shaughnessy as city engineer and charged him with developing a water system based on bringing water from the Sierra Nevada and with developing a streetcar system to open up the western parts of the city to residential development. O'Shaughnessy was up to the task. A graduate of the Royal University of Dublin, he was known nationally as a leading hydraulic engineer.

When O'Shaughnessy began work in 1912, the city was about to celebrate the opening of the first municipally owned streetcar line in any major city. O'Shaughnessy quickly drafted plans for new streetcar lines to serve the PPIE, and voters approved a bond issue in August 1913. Construction began immediately. By opening day of the exposition, February 20, 1915, one new line carried passengers from the working-class South of Market area to the exposition; a second new line, on Stockton

Street, connected the downtown shopping district to the PPIE via a new tunnel under a steep hill; and there were several other new lines that had been designed and built in the previous twenty-nine months. O'Shaughnessy then turned to extending the Municipal Railway into other areas, including the Mission District and the largely undeveloped sand dunes of the outer Sunset, Parkside, and Ingleside districts. The Twin Peaks Tunnel, the longest streetcar tunnel in the world when it opened in 1917, provided service to the southwestern quarter of the city. Between 1915 and 1927, O'Shaughnessy pushed to completion the heart of San Francisco's present streetcar system, the J, K, L, M, and N lines.

O'Shaughnessy envisioned a single streetcar system that could provide a uniform level of service at a reasonable price throughout the city. He also saw the streetcar system as a way to encourage and manage growth by extending new lines into undeveloped areas. Equally important to O'Shaughnessy's vision was cost-effectiveness derived from careful design rather than low wages. For O'Shaughnessy, efficiency and cost-effectiveness resulted from keeping all operations free from political influence. As city engineer, O'Shaughnessy also oversaw creation of the new high-pressure fire system, new sewers, boulevards and highways, tunnels, and more.

However, it was Hetch Hetchy that had convinced O'Shaughnessy to leave a lucrative private practice and accept a reduced salary to design and build one of the nation's most ambitious water systems. In December 1913, Congress approved damming the Hetch Hetchy Valley in Yosemite National Park. The project involved building the main dam, a 68-mile-long railroad to the dam; several smaller dams; a 156-mile-long aqueduct that included 85 miles of tunnels, some through solid granite; and hydroelectric generating plants and transmission lines. An initial bond issue of $45 million, approved in 1910, was exhausted before the work was half done, requiring additional bond issues in the 1920s. The total cost, from the first surveys to the time when Hetch Hetchy water flowed from city faucets, was about $100 million (equivalent to $2.3 billion in 2024), and O'Shaughnessy took great pride that, as he put it, "not a crooked finger had been able to chisel a dollar out of it." In 1934, sixteen days after O'Shaughnessy died of a heart attack, the first water from Hetch Hetchy reached San Francisco.

Moral Reform

Although the saloons, gambling houses, and brothels of the Barbary Coast had burned in 1906, such establishments were quickly rebuilt. In 1911, under the administration of Mayor McCarthy, the Municipal Clinic opened, and prostitutes were required to have regular medical examinations and to have any disease treated. The Municipal Clinic significantly reduced venereal disease but was highly controversial as contributing to immorality. Rolph initially supported the clinic. but then reversed position. The clinic closed, and disease again spread throughout the Barbary Coast district.

Progressive reformers joined with conservative clergymen in an effort to close down all brothels. Despite arguments that closing the brothels would mean that prostitutes would scatter throughout the city, progressives and religious leaders continued to crusade against prostitution. Finally, in early 1917, Mayor Rolph directed police to close the Barbary Coast brothels. When prostitutes dispersed throughout the city, a police morals squad was created, but it had only limited success in suppressing prostitution.

Changing Demography and Geography

The new Municipal Railway streetcar lines were not the city's only streetcar lines. Older cable-car and electric streetcar lines were still operating and had been consolidated by the Market Street Railway (MSR). Some MSR lines offered streetcar service to the western half of San Francisco, which was developing as residential areas in the late nineteenth and early twentieth centuries. By 1915, residential construction had filled in the Inner Sunset and Inner Richmond neighborhoods, but much of the rest of the western part of the city still consisted of sand dunes.

Figure 6.4 indicates the ethnic composition of the city's population as of the 1910 census. San Francisco remained a city of immigrants, with more than two-thirds of the city's population either first- or second-generation immigrants, nearly all from Europe. Immigration from Italy and Russia had increased significantly. There were proportionately fewer of Chinese parentage, but more immigrants from Japan.

The number of Italian immigrants doubled between 1900 and 1910, then almost tripled between 1910 and 1920. By 1910 or so, North

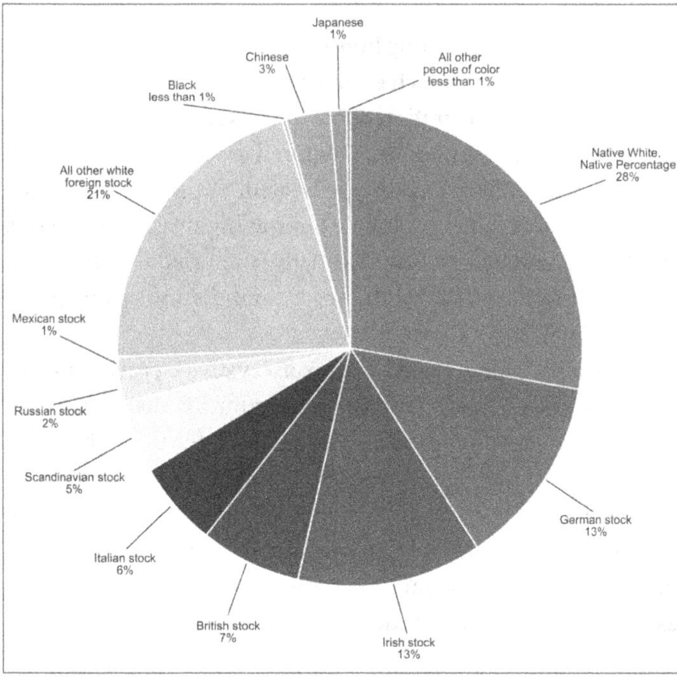

Figure 6.4. San Francisco ethnicity and race based on 1910 census data.

Beach had become home to many Italian immigrants and their children, as well as Italian businesses. Among the most successful was the Bank of Italy, founded in 1904 by Amadeo P. Giannini, then a successful produce merchant. In 1906, Giannini had been able to load the bank's entire stock of cash into a wagon and take it his home in San Mateo County before the fires reached his bank. In the immediate aftermath of the fire, his was one of the first banks to open for business. The Bank of Italy then became a pioneer in branch banking. At a time when banks operated from one location, in or near the financial district, Giannini began to open branch banks, first in 1907 in the Mission District, then in San Jose in 1919, Los Angeles in 1913, and in many of San Francisco's neighborhoods in the 1920s.

Some immigrants faced strong opposition. By the early twentieth century, new arrivals from Japan were attracting the attention of opponents of Chinese immigration. In 1905, union leaders formed the Asiatic Exclusion League, calling for an end to all immigration from Asia and for school segregation. In the aftermath of the destruction of 1906, the city's school board ordered Japanese students, most of whom lived in the Western Addition, to attend the Chinese school, which was far away in Chinatown. The Japanese government, which had recently humiliated a white European nation in the Russo-Japanese War, was outraged over this insult to their nationals. After President Theodore Roosevelt brought the school board to Washington for talks, the board rescinded the segregation order. Roosevelt then negotiated the so-called Gentlemen's Agreement of 1907 between the US and Japan, by which Japan agreed to significantly reduce immigration to the US.

The Japanese school incident came as the segregation of Chinese students was beginning to break down. In 1905, a student of Chinese ancestry sought to attend high school. The school board was caught between its commitment to segregation and the need to increase taxes to build a separate high school. Taxes trumped racism, and Chinese students were admitted to existing high schools. At the same time, more Chinese families were living away from Chinatown, and by 1919 some Chinese students were enrolled in neighborhood elementary schools.

Nonetheless, anti-Asian rhetoric remained a staple for many white political figures, progressives and conservatives alike. Governor Hiram Johnson joined Theodore Roosevelt's Progressive Party in the 1912 presidential election as candidate for vice president. Phelan, in support of Woodrow Wilson, accused Roosevelt of being insufficiently hostile to Japanese immigration, and Wilson narrowly carried California and won the presidency. The following year, Johnson and his supporters in the state legislature passed a state law prohibiting persons ineligible for citizenship (Asians) from owning property. Phelan won election to the US Senate in 1914, on a strongly anti-Asian platform, accusing Asian immigrants of endangering white civilization. His slogan when he ran for reelection in 1920 was "Keep California White."

World War I and the Influenza Pandemic

The PPIE had the great misfortune to open in 1915. By then, much of Europe had gone to war. Of the leading combatants, Great Britain, Germany, and Russia did not have exhibits. The US entered World War I in spring 1917.

Figure 6.5. Hamilton Henry Dobbin, the photographer, may have staged this scene of a man being arrested for not wearing a mask during the 1918 influenza epidemic in San Francisco. Dobbin was himself a police officer. The text written under the photo is "Ah! Come on & Tell it to the Judge." Photo from the Dobbin Collection, courtesy the California State Library.

The influenza pandemic in 1918 and 1919 came as World War I was ending. The pandemic killed 20–40 million people worldwide, including 500,000–675,000 Americans. When the first surge of infections came to San Francisco, in September 1918, city officials specified that anyone not wearing a gauze face mask would be subject to fines ranging from five dollars to one hundred dollars (five dollars in 1918 was equivalent to more than one hundred dollars in 2025) and the possibility of ten days' imprisonment. The rules were enforced—even Mayor Rolph was fined fifty dollars. The city closed its dance halls, theaters, movie houses, and schools, and prohibited large gatherings. Nonetheless, by the end of October, San Francisco had experienced a total of nearly twenty thousand cases of influenza and over one thousand deaths. When the number of cases tapered off in November, the city relaxed its restrictions. Then a second surge came in January 1919, and city officials again ordered people to wear masks in public. This time, more than two thousand people held a public protest against the mask mandate. By the end of the second surge, the city recorded nearly forty-five thousand cases, almost 10 percent of the population, and more than three thousand deaths, among the highest death rates of major US cities.

By the spring of 1919, the war was over, and the influenza pandemic had passed. By then, the nation had passed through not only its first war in Europe, but also nearly two decades when progressive reforms had dominated national, state, and local politics.

PORTFOLIO B

The Earthquake and Fire of 1906

Before, During, and After

BEFORE THE EARTHQUAKE

Figure B.1. The "New" City Hall, 1905, constructed between 1870 and 1897. Photo originally published in *New International Encyclopedia*, 1905, courtesy Wikimedia Commons.

Figure B.2. Looking west on Market Street from the tower of the Ferry Building, ca. 1896. The Spreckels Building can be seen in the distance. Photo AAB-4919, courtesy the San Francisco History Center, San Francisco Public Library.

Figure B.3. Market Street in flames, April 19, 1906. US Army troops are patrolling in foreground. Photo H26.2518d, courtesy Oakland Museum of California.

Figure B.4. Third day of the fire. People are watching the city burn in the distance. Photographer unknown, courtesy the National Archives.

Figure B.5. Ruins of City Hall. Photograph by George Williford Boyce Haley, courtesy the Library of Congress.

Figure B.6. Looking west on Market Street from the Ferry Building, April 1906. The Spreckels Building and a few other steel-frame buildings can be seen above the rubble. Photo WNP24.189, courtesy OpenSF/History.

Figure B.7. The Presidio's chief nurse, Dora Thompson, stands in front of Army Field Hospital No. 1 in Golden Gate Park. The army supplied field kitchens, field hospitals, and tents for the refugees from the earthquake and fire. Photo GOGA 35256 courtesy Park Archives, Golden Gate National Recreation Area.

Figure B.8. Army tents were set up in open spaces around the city. This tent city was one of several in Golden Gate Park. Photo WNP15.1083, courtesy OpenSFHistory.

Figure B.9. Union carpenters pose for the photographer at a camp in the Richmond District, between Geary and Lake Streets, east of 14th Avenue. Some 5,600 small cottages, usually called earthquake shacks, were assembled in parks and other open spaces around the city, replacing the tents. Residents paid two dollars per month in rent. When their rent reached fifty dollars, they owned the shack. Photo from collection of Jesse B. Cook, courtesy of California Historical Society Collection at Stanford University.

Figure B.10. Moving day! Residents of the earthquake shacks who became owners were required to move their cottage onto a permanent site. At last count, some thirty are still in use as residences. This marked a major increase in homeownership among San Franciscans of moderate income, at least in the short term. Photo AAC-2848, courtesy the San Francisco History Center, San Francisco Public Library.

Figure B.11. The new San Francisco City Hall was designed by Arthur Brown Jr., in French Renaissance style and constructed between 1913 and 1915. Photo CHS2015.2010, courtesy the California Historical Society.

Figure B.12. Market Street, looking west from the Ferry Building, 1913. Photo WNP26.1156, courtesy OpenSFHistory.

CELEBRATING THE RECOVERY: THE PANAMA-PACIFIC INTERNATIONAL EXPOSITION, 1915

Figure B.13. Tower of Jewels, Panama Pacific International Exposition, 1915. Photo courtesy Wikimedia Commons.

Figure B.14. Large numbers of people came for Opening Day festivities at the Panama Pacific Exposition, February 20, 1915. Photo AAD-7041 courtesy the San Francisco History Center, San Francisco Public Library.

7

Prosperity, Depression, and War, 1920–45

By 1920, some San Franciscans, like many Americans, heaved a sigh of relief after the many changes introduced by progressivism, the dangers of the war, and the pressures of the influenza pandemic. The election of the bland, conservative Warren G. Harding as president in 1920 along with constitutional amendments enacting woman suffrage and Prohibition signaled an end to most progressive reform at the national level.

Reflecting on the Roaring Twenties today usually conjures images of a booming economy and people dancing the Charleston while swigging bootleg liquor. San Franciscans shared in the economic boom, danced the Charleston, and drank bootleg liquor, but the boom ended with a crash in 1929, initiating the Great Depression, which brought major changes to the city. And the Depression was followed by war.

The 1920s: Economic Growth, Labor Conflict, and a New Charter

During the 1920s, the city's economy grew in much the same patterns established earlier. Comparing 1919 to 1929, the manufacturing sector was stable, with the largest numbers of workers in food processing, especially meatpacking, fruit and vegetable canning, and coffee roasting and canning. Next in size came publishing (both of books and periodicals) and metalworking, including foundries, machine-shop production, and shipbuilding. Shipbuilding had boomed during World War I but declined just as sharply when the war ended. By 1929, some forty-five thousand people were employed in manufacturing, down from forty-eight thousand at the end of the war, but up by almost a third from before the war.

The Board of State Harbor Commissioners declared San Francisco "the great American hub of trade on the Pacific," and the port continued as the heart of the city's economy, handling more than ten million tons of cargo each year. Port facilities expanded during the 1920s, stretching over nearly six miles by 1929. The 1930 census listed some twenty-six thousand workers in "transportation," the largest number of them in maritime commerce: on the docks, on ships, in warehouses, as teamsters, in ship repair, on the state-owned railway line that ran along the Embarcadero (the broad thoroughfare in front of the docks), and elsewhere. Much of the city's manufacturing depended on the port: coffee beans arrived from Central America, raw sugar from Hawaii, steel and automobile parts from Baltimore. Fruit and vegetables for canning came by boat from the Central Valley. Some of the city's manufacturing depended on the port to ship finished products, notably canned goods going to the East Coast. The value of the cargo handled by the port ranked second only to New York in the nation, though in tonnage San Francisco ranked lower.

The expansion of the national economy in the 1920s was based in significant part on housing construction and sales of such consumer goods as automobiles and new electric appliances, especially radios. In addition to innovating with branch banks, Giannini's Bank of Italy pioneered in encouraging working people to open accounts and to borrow for car purchases—something virtually unknown previously. By 1920, the Bank of Italy was the largest bank in California, and it became the third largest in the nation in 1927. Giannini renamed it the Bank of America in 1930.

Housing construction boomed in the 1920s, producing more rowhouses and flats, along with many apartment buildings, throughout the mid-Sunset, mid-Richmond, and outer Mission neighborhoods, and also in the new Marina District, on the site of the PPIE. That decade also saw construction of upper-income housing in the city's residential parks, including Forest Hill, St. Francis Wood, and Ingleside Terrace, most initiated before World War I. All the residential parks were exclusively residential, with only single-family, detached houses, curvilinear streets, and sometimes private parks. All were well served by new streetcar lines, and most included racial covenants, restricting property ownership to whites or, as in one example, prohibiting ownership by anyone of "African, Japanese, Chinese, or any Mongolian descent." Unlike some cities, there were no restrictions on Catholics or Jews.

In the 1920s, for the first time, the city adopted formal city planning procedures and policies. In 1912, voters had approved a charter amendment creating the planning commission. However, little in the way of new policies appeared until 1921 when the commission proposed and the Board of Supervisors approved dividing the city into six zoning districts: single dwellings, group dwellings (flats and apartment houses), commercial (stores and office buildings), light industrial, heavy industrial, and "unrestricted." In approving the policy, the supervisors gave special attention to drawing the new zoning district boundaries in a way designed to prevent the city's Japanese neighborhood from expanding.

Throughout the 1920s, under O'Shaughnessy's direction, the Municipal Railway extended its lines. Construction of the complex Hetch Hetchy system also proceeded, but the final steps were never realized. The Pacific Gas and Electric Company was repeatedly successful in defeating bond issues to bring electrical power from the Hetch Hetchy system directly to San Franciscans' homes. Voters also defeated bond issues to buy out the city's privately owned streetcar lines.

The economic expansion of the 1920s, both nationally and in San Francisco, was unlike previous periods of growth in the 1880s and early 1900s in that unions declined rather than grew. Nationally and in San Francisco, this resulted from strong anti-union drives by employers in the absence of legal protections for labor organizations. Some of the largest union organizations in San Francisco were defeated. First, in 1919, the Riggers and Stevedores, the union of longshoremen (those who loaded and unloaded ships), was beaten after a long strike. Next the Metal Trades Council, representing workers in shipyards and foundries, was defeated. In 1921, shipboard workers' unions, including the Sailors' Union of the Pacific, lost a nationwide strike. In 1921, the San Francisco Building Trades Council, one of the most powerful union organizations in the country, also met defeat.

The Building Trades Council was defeated by a Citizens' Committee, formed when the Chamber of Commerce raised a $1 million fund (equivalent to more than $17 million in 2025) from the city's banks, railroads, shipping companies, oil companies, and other businesses to support the employers and fight the unions. The Citizens' Committee transitioned into the Industrial Association of San Francisco, committed to what it called the American Plan. Also called the open shop, it meant that employers refused to recognize unions as representing workers and that only employers were to determine working conditions. Throughout the 1920s and early 1930s, the Industrial Association dominated labor relations. Only a few unions survived with their membership and contracts intact. A US Senate investigating committee later described the Industrial Association as exercising "complete dominance of organized labor" and as "a model of militant employer tactics."

Many in the city's business community also came together to urge charter reform, to structure city government more like a business corporation. In 1930, voters elected a Board of Freeholders to write a new city charter. The new charter was approved by voters with the strongest support from upper- and middle-class neighborhoods. Under the new charter, the mayor continued as the city's chief executive and was responsible for appointing the new positions of city administrator and controller. The city administrator supervised a wide range of activities, including health, public works, and taxes and assessments. The controller was responsible for the budget. The number of supervisors was reduced from eighteen to eleven, elected at large. The mayor also appointed members of citizen commissions, responsible for such things as planning, the library system, and public utilities.

Rolph presided over city government throughout most of the 1920s, although he no longer exhibited the initiative and drive of his early years. In 1930, he won election as governor and resigned the mayoralty. The Board of Supervisors chose Angelo Rossi, one of its members and a successful florist, to succeed Rolph. Rossi, the city's first mayor of Italian descent, won election on his own later that year.

The City in Crisis: The Great Depression and the Strikes of 1934

The stock market crashed in October 1929, setting off an economic contraction that became more and more extreme. The Great Depression lasted more than ten years, although the economy improved somewhat after 1933. Manufacturing companies reduced production in response to reduced demand. Fewer ships came to the port. Unemployment grew. Those without work became eligible for work-relief: a week's labor on some city project brought a family a three-week supply of groceries. In 1929, some 1,700 families received relief each month. The demand soon outstripped city funds, but voters approved bond issues in 1931 and 1932 to continue relief programs. By 1933, some 18,000 families were receiving relief—almost 10 percent of all families, concentrated among blue-collar wage-earners. The city's peak unemployment reached 32 percent.

New city construction provided some jobs. In 1927, voters approved a bond issue to construct the War Memorial complex, including an opera house and a veterans' building, the latter with offices for veterans' organizations on the lower floor and an art museum on the upper floor. Construction got under way in 1931 as the Depression deepened. A long-discussed bridge from San Francisco to Oakland had moved to the planning stage in 1929 when President Herbert Hoover, a Californian, and Governor C. C. Young appointed a joint commission. With a loan from the federal Reconstruction Finance Administration (the Hoover administration's major effort to restore the devastated economy), construction began in 1933 and was completed in 1936. In 1930, voters in San Francisco and the counties to its north approved a bond issue to build a bridge across the Golden Gate. Construction began in 1933 and was complete in 1937. City voters also approved a major bond issue to build or remodel public school buildings.

However, local work-relief programs and public construction failed to restore the city's economy. In the early 1930s, amid growing unemployment, the city's small Communist Party mobilized thousands of people in demonstrations against unemployment. On the waterfront, longshoremen began to agitate for a new union, one group led by a conservative and another composed of militants, some with connections to the Communist Party. Similar organizing of longshore workers was going on in other Pacific Coast ports.

In the 1932 presidential election, Franklin D. Roosevelt, the Democrat, swept to victory, winning almost two-thirds of the vote in San Francisco. Upon taking office in March 1933, he summoned Congress into special session. Within a hundred days, Roosevelt and Congress wrote into law the first New Deal, intended to reverse the economic paralysis, initiate economic reforms, provide relief for the unemployed, and end Prohibition. One provision specified that "employees shall have the right to organize and bargain collectively through representatives of their own choosing," launching a nationwide boom in union organizing.

In July 1933, a new local of the International Longshoremen's Association (ILA) was chartered in San Francisco. By late 1933, ILA locals in all the Pacific Coast ports had formulated bargaining demands, foremost among them a union hiring hall to guarantee that jobs would be apportioned fairly among all union members. Employers refused to bargain and accused the union of being dominated by Communists. On May 9, 1934, more than ten thousand ILA members went on strike from northern Washington to Southern California, trying to shut down Pacific Coast shipping. As ships entered Pacific Coast ports, their crews quickly went on strike with issues of their own, adding more than six thousand maritime workers to the number on strike. Most teamsters refused to move cargoes unloaded by strikebreakers. San Francisco—the largest port on the Pacific Coast and location of the corporate headquarters of most shipping companies—was the center of the strike. Harry Bridges, an Australian immigrant and chairman of the strike committee for the San Francisco ILA local, rapidly emerged as de facto leader of the local and, increasingly, for the entire coastwise strike.

Waterfront employers in San Francisco hired a thousand strikebreakers to work the ships, hoping to defeat the union. The strikebreakers could unload cargo, but the striking union members were able to prevent most of it from leaving the piers. Federal officials from the Department of Labor tried to bring a settlement, but neither side was willing to give in on the hiring hall. In mid-June, the national president of the ILA brokered a settlement, but it was rejected by ILA members because it lacked a union hiring hall. In San Francisco, waterfront employers turned to the Industrial Association, which began preparations to break the strike by using nonunion truck drivers to take cargo off the docks.

In the afternoon of July 3, the Industrial Association put its plans into action behind a massive barricade of police cars, police on horseback, and police on foot. The next workday, July 5, thousands of strikers and strike supporters faced the police barricades. In midmorning, police wielding riot guns, tear gas, and riot clubs began to clear the southern waterfront of protestors. Police gunfire killed two and wounded more than twenty strikers and five bystanders. More than a hundred people were injured by police gunfire, clubs, or tear gas. Among Pacific Coast longshore workers, July 5 is still remembered as Bloody Thursday.

The governor sent in the National Guard, with machine guns and tanks, to patrol the waterfront and protect strikebreakers. On July 9, a funeral for the two slain men was followed by a dramatic funeral procession that filled Market Street for more than two miles. One newspaper estimated seven thousand marchers; another estimated fifteen thousand. Angela Gizzi, daughter of Italian immigrants, left work to stand in respect during the dramatic funeral march down Market Street. She recalled, "it was the most spectacular thing I've ever seen. . . . that's how I became a radical."

The Labor Council, central body for all the city's unions, created a General Strike Committee that designated Monday, July 16, as the first day of a general strike in support of the striking maritime unions and in protest against police violence and the National Guard. Nearly all union members stopped work. No taxis or trucks moved. Movie theaters, barbershops, dry cleaners, bars, auto-repair shops, and most gas stations were closed. Many small businesses in working-class neighborhoods also closed. Panic-stricken civic and business leaders thought the general strike was a Communist revolution. Vigilantes—never identified—roamed the city and surrounding areas, breaking into the offices of leftist organizations, especially those linked to the Communist Party. The vigilantes broke up furniture and equipment

CAROLYN ANSPACHER REPORTS FROM THE HARBOR EMERGENCY HOSPITAL, JULY 5, 1934

Carolyn Anspacher wrote this report for the *San Francisco Chronicle*:

> San Francisco's broad Embarcadero ran red with blood yesterday and the Harbor Emergency Hospital stood a small haven for the injured.
>
> Here all were treated . . . strikers, strikebreakers, police, guardsmen, casual passers-by, news reporters and photographers . . . Here all were treated with the same efficiency and speed . . .
>
> In times of stress a hospital, particularly an emergency hospital, has a psychology all its own. . . . It catches the pulse of the conflict . . . the many pulses, really . . . and welds them into one. Into a pounding, surging pulse that yesterday beat STRIKE . . . STRIKE! . . . each word was a symphony of blood.
>
> Drip-drip-drip went the blood on the white tiled floor. Steadily. Drip-drip-drip. Human blood, bright as red begonias in the sun. . . .
>
> Most of us who made that hospital our headquarters yesterday came to hate the sight of red. . . .
>
> There was so much of it.
>
> The color stained clothing, sheets, human flesh.
>
> Some of it was blood . . . some antiseptic. It all looked the same. It was the color of the strike . . .

Anspacher, then in her mid-twenties, had joined the *Chronicle* the year before, after her wealthy family lost much of their money in the Great Depression. At that time, women reporters were usually assigned to cover society weddings and similar social events, but one of Anspacher's first reports was on a violent lynching in San Jose. She later said, "Newspaper writing became not only my bread but my wine," and that "it was so exciting, so unpredictable, so fascinating." She remained a *Chronicle* reporter for more than fifty years, until shortly before her death, often the only woman other than those doing the "women's" section. When she died, the *Chronicle* editors said, "She wrote with elegance, dispatch, and, often, fury." But in all her years of reporting, nothing quite matched the amount of blood she saw on July 5, 1934.

Figure 7.1. National Guard tanks and machine guns protected the strikebreakers working on the San Francisco docks in July 1934. Photo AAD-5113 courtesy the San Francisco History Center, San Francisco Public Library.

and beat anyone inside. When the vigilantes left, police arrived to arrest those who had been beaten.

The General Strike Committee ended the strike after four days. By its end, waterfront employers had agreed to arbitration. Longshore and maritime workers also agreed to arbitration and returned to work at the end of July. Through arbitration by a board appointed by President Roosevelt, longshore workers received better pay and shorter hours. They did not get a union hiring hall but got the next best thing—a dispatcher elected by ILA members. Harry Bridges was soon elected president of the San Francisco ILA local, and then as president of the Pacific Coast District of the ILA.

From late 1936 through early 1937, another strike by all longshore and maritime unions shut down Pacific Coast ports for three months.

Figure 7.2. Harry Bridges with the ILWU contingent in the 1939 Labor Day Parade on Market Street in San Francisco. Photo courtesy the Anne Rand Research Library, International Longshore and Warehouse Union.

It was, however, the last such joint strike by all the maritime unions. In mid-1937, the Pacific Coast ILA joined the new Congress of Industrial Organizations (CIO) as the International Longshoremen's and Warehousemen's Union (ILWU), with Bridges as its president. Some maritime unions also joined the CIO, but others stayed with the American Federation of Labor. Conflict between the CIO and AFL meant that union members at times fought each other as bitterly as they had fought the companies. Employers and patriotic organizations joined with immigration officials in claiming that Bridges was a Communist and seeking to deport him. An initial hearing in 1939 found for Bridges, but a second hearing in 1941 went against him, leading to appeals all the way to the US Supreme Court, which found for Bridges in 1945.

By the mid-1930s, San Francisco had regained its reputation as a union town, as new federal legislation protected unions and encouraged collective bargaining as the way to resolve labor disputes.

Federal Programs for Relief and Recovery

In addition to labor legislation, Roosevelt's New Deal included relief for the unemployed and programs to stimulate the economy through

SAN FRANCISCANS APPEAL TO THE US SUPREME COURT: HARRY BRIDGES (1941) AND WILLIAM SCHNEIDERMAN (1943)

In the late 1930s and early 1940s, two San Franciscans were involved in precedent-setting cases before the US Supreme Court, both involving the rights of immigrants.

Harry Bridges, a native of Australia who had not completed his naturalization, appealed to the Supreme Court when a state judge in Los Angeles found him in contempt of court for releasing to the press a telegram critical of the judge that Bridges had sent to the secretary of labor. Bridges appealed, eventually all the way to the US Supreme Court, which in 1941 decided in his favor, citing freedom of speech. The decision in *Bridges v. California* was only the second time the court had invoked the Fourteenth Amendment as limiting the ability of state or local governments to infringe upon the liberties in the First Amendment, but more such decisions followed. The decision in *Bridges v. California* also set the precedent that the rights guaranteed by the Fourteenth Amendment applied to "people" (the language of the Fourteenth Amendment), and not only to citizens.

William Schneiderman was born in Russia in 1905 and came to the US with his parents in 1908. At sixteen, Schneiderman joined the youth program of the Communist Party (CP). He became a citizen in 1927. In 1939, when he was head of the CP in California, federal prosecutors brought him to trial seeking to revoke his citizenship on the grounds that he had denied being a member of the CP when he became a citizen and that CP membership was sufficient grounds to revoke citizenship. The trial judge ruled against Schneiderman. His attorneys appealed, eventually to the US Supreme Court.

In late 1941, in a surprise that made the front page of the *New York Times*, Wendell Willkie joined Schneiderman's defense team and agreed to argue his case before the Supreme Court. Willkie had been the Republican candidate for president in 1940. Schneiderman's attorneys had argued that Schneiderman had committed no fraud because the 1927 naturalization forms did not ask about CP membership. Willkie saw a broader issue: the Schneiderman case had the potential to affect every naturalized citizen.

The Supreme Court's decision, in 1943, was that the government had failed to show by "an exacting standard of proof" that the CP was committed to the overthrow of the government by force and violence, and that the views of Communist theoreticians or leaders could not be imputed to Schneiderman without specific evidence.

The decision in *Schneiderman v. U.S.* established the precedent that "clear, unequivocal, and convincing evidence" must be proven in order to remove a person's citizenship. This strict standard of evidence significantly reduced the number of denaturalization prosecutions. The decision also produced the general proposition that the unlawful purposes of an organization do not warrant deprivation of its members' rights without evidence of the members' knowledge of those purposes and their specific intent to further them. The decision has been cited in thousands of cases, especially its evocation of the need for "clear, unequivocal, and convincing evidence."

Figure 7.3. This postcard from 1940 seems to present opening day at San Francisco's Aquatic Park, a joint project of the city and the WPA. The park included the bathhouse (now the Maritime Museum, the large building in center right), the viewing stands filled with people (to the left of the bathhouse), other structures, and a breakwater (not visible). Photo P17–005.4P (SAFR 24860) courtesy the National Park Service, San Francisco Maritime National Historic Park.

construction of infrastructure. During the winter of 1933–34, the new Civil Works Administration (CWA) hired eight thousand unemployed San Franciscans for projects ranging from gardening in city parks and creating new streets to building new playgrounds and rehabilitating public buildings. Unemployed musicians were organized into a CWA orchestra, and unemployed artists created bold murals in public buildings.

When CWA ended, some of its programs were continued by the State Emergency Relief Administration. A new federal work-relief program, the Works Progress Administration (WPA), took over in 1935 and continued until World War II. Mayor Rossi secured WPA funding for a wide variety of projects that employed thousands of San Franciscans: building or widening streets and sidewalks, building bridges and overpasses, creating O'Shaughnessy Boulevard, and constructing approaches to the two new bridges. They worked in city parks; expanded the zoo; created Aquatic Park; remodeled or expanded city buildings; and constructed playgrounds, recreation centers, and two branch libraries. A WPA writers program produced several publications, including a city guidebook that included nearly every neighborhood—not just the tourist attractions. The CWA orchestra continued under WPA.

The CWA and WPA provided work-relief to the unemployed. Another New Deal program, the Public Works Administration (PWA), sought to stimulate the economy through major construction projects. In San Francisco, PWA helped to fund twelve new school buildings, remodeling or expansion of other school buildings, three new federal buildings including a new mint, new construction at the port, two new city buildings including the Cow Palace, a major expansion of O'Shaughnessy Dam, a new sewage treatment plant for the Sunset and Richmond districts, and several public housing projects. A new bulk-mail facility, the Rincon Annex Post Office, was built on Mission Street near the port.

San Francisco also gained a rich collection of public art through New Deal programs. Under the Public Works of Art Project of the CWA, fifty artists and assistants painted all the walls on the first and second floors of the new Coit Memorial Tower. Most used the color palette and worked in the style of the Mexican muralist Diego Rivera. Later, under the Federal Art Project of the WPA, Lucien Labaudt depicted city life, especially recreation, on all the first-floor walls of the Beach Chalet, and Victor Arnautoff painted thirteen panels on the Life and Era of George Washington at the new George Washington High School. Sargent Johnson, one of the few New Deal artists in San Francisco who identified as Black, sculpted a spectacular bas-relief mural of athletes for that school's athletic field. Hilaire Hiler created a surreal view of undersea life for what is now the Maritime Museum, and Sargent Johnson added surreal bas-relief sculptures and mosaics outside the building. Dorothy Puccinelli and Helen Forbes wrapped large murals around the upper interior of the Mothers Building at the zoo, presenting the story of Noah's ark with colorful depictions of animals; Margaret, Esther, and Helen Bruton created mosaic murals on the exterior of that building. The Mothers Building may be the largest New Deal art project entirely by women anywhere in the country. Another New Deal arts program, through the Treasury Department, commissioned murals by Anton Refregier on the history of California, especially San Francisco, in what is now Rincon Center. Refregier's murals constitute the largest New Deal art project anywhere by a single artist. And there were more. The murals, nearly all of which survive, are perhaps the best known of the many New Deal projects that remain throughout the city.

In 1939–40, the city celebrated the completion of the two great bridges and the opening of airplane passenger service across the Pacific with the Golden Gate International Exposition, held on Treasure Island, an artificial island created in the middle of the Bay through assistance from several federal agencies. The long-term plan was for Treasure Island to become the city's airport. In the short term, it was transformed by exhibition halls. The entire exposition was filled with art done by artists working through the WPA arts program, and, in 1940, a special program, Art in Action, featured WPA artists creating works in view of visitors to the exposition, most of which were slated to become part of the new campus then under construction for San Francisco Junior College, now City College of San Francisco.

The highlight of Art in Action was a massive mural by Diego Rivera, who agreed to come to San Francisco if private donors would cover his expenses. His assistants were paid by WPA. Rivera's huge mural—twenty-two feet high and seventy-four feet long—presents a sweeping synthesis of the art, religion, history, politics, and technology of the Americas.

CWA, WPA, and PWA funds also flowed to the Presidio, which had been expanded in previous years to include artillery installations all around the entrance to the Bay, making it one of the most heavily fortified areas on the planet. In the late 1930s, as international tensions rose, WPA and PWA funds were used for new barracks and officers' housing and for a major remodeling of Letterman Hospital, the army's major medical facility for operations in the Pacific.

World War II

The artillery around the Golden Gate were never tested in actual combat, but, by 1941, wars were raging in East Asia, where Japanese forces had overrun much of eastern China, and in Europe, where Germany and its ally Italy had overrun much of western and southern Europe. Germany and Italy were opposed by Britain and, after mid-1941, the Soviet Union. War came to the US on December 7, 1941, when a Japanese fleet attacked US Navy ships at Pearl Harbor, in Hawaii, and then took the Philippine Islands. The US soon found itself facing war both in Europe and in the Pacific. The Presidio of San Francisco played a major role in the war in the Pacific. Instead of becoming the city's airport, Treasure Island became a navy base.

The army divided the nation into four defense commands. The Presidio housed headquarters for the Western Defense Command, covering all the states west of the Rockies. The Presidio also served as a major training center. For example, the Presidio's School for Bakers and Cooks trained soldiers in dietetics, sanitation, and quality food preparation and also produced two thousand loaves of bread every day for Bay Area military facilities. Fort Mason was the major embarkation point for troops and supplies headed into the Pacific. Letterman Hospital, at the Presidio, served as the major hospital for treating the wounded and sick from the Pacific. Toward the end of the war, so many hospital ships were arriving that a rail line was built from the docks at Fort Mason to Letterman Hospital to transport the wounded. In the last year of the war, seventy-two thousand patients passed through Letterman's doors.

Before Pearl Harbor, the Presidio was also site of a highly secret Military Intelligence Service language school. Beginning in September 1941, the army began to identify soldiers, mostly Nisei (born in the US of Japanese-born parents), with Japanese language skills. They went to the Presidio to receive extensive training in Japanese language, culture, and military terminology so they could serve as army translators—to help to interrogate prisoners, issue propaganda, and translate documents. The school was moved to Minnesota the next year when army was removing and interning all persons of Japanese ancestry on the Pacific Coast.

KARL YONEDA JOINS THE US ARMY, 1942

Karl Yoneda was born Goso Yoneda in 1906 to immigrant parents from Japan. He lived in Japan from 1913 to 1926, where he attended school and became interested in socialism. He joined the Communist Party under the name Karl (for Marx) shortly after he returned to the US. In 1933, he became editor of *Rodo Shimbun* (Labor News), the Communist Party's Japanese-language newspaper, in San Francisco. In early 1936, he helped organize the Alaska Cannery Workers Union, composed of Mexican, Filipino, Chinese, and Japanese workers who shipped to Alaska each summer to work in the fish canneries. Yoneda was elected as delegate to the San Francisco Labor Council, which had long banned locals that enrolled Asians. He broke that long-standing barrier and became the first Asian to serve on that body.

Yoneda tried to enlist in the army immediately after Pearl Harbor but was not accepted. He later recalled, "I was greatly disappointed but determined more than ever to pursue the right to enlist." Instead, he, his wife (who was not Japanese), and their three-year-old son were sent to Manzanar, one of the internment camps. When recruiters from the Military Intelligence Service came to Manzanar, Yoneda encouraged others to join him enlisting; he later recalled that he'd told them, "this was the opportune time to fight against the fascist Axis which was the main enemy of democratic people everywhere. Enlisting was the best way to guarantee and protect our future." He was accepted into the army and sent to the Military Intelligence Service language school in Minnesota. Yoneda's proficiency in written as well as spoken Japanese made him a valuable asset for the army. He was promoted to sergeant and sent to the China-India-Burma theater, where US and British forces were opening the Burma Road into southern China to supply Chinese forces fighting the Japanese. Among other duties, Yoneda wrote leaflets calling upon Japanese troops to surrender and broadcast similar messages.

After the war, Karl worked as a longshoreman and was a member of ILWU Local 10. After retiring, he authored several books on Asian labor history in the US; a memoir, *Ganbatte: Sixty-Year Struggle of a Kibei Worker* (1983); and *A Nikkei M.I.S. Soldier's Diary, 1942–1945* (published in Japan, 1989).

In the immediate aftermath of Pearl Harbor, fear of a possible Japanese invasion gripped the city. All city lights throughout the state were turned off at night. A great net was hung under the Golden Gate Bridge to prevent submarines from entering the Bay, and barbed wire was set up on beaches near the Presidio. These precautions were not entirely unfounded; submarines from Japan did sink several ships near the California coast, and one shelled an oil refinery close to Santa Barbara.

Amid this panic, California newspapers and radio commentators began to present Japanese Americans as potentially disloyal and dangerous. The press, Governor Culbert Olson, and California Attorney General Earl Warren lobbied for removal of all people of Japanese ancestry. On February 19, 1942, President Roosevelt signed Executive Order 9066, authorizing the secretary of war to designate military areas from which "any or all persons may be excluded." The order never specified "Japanese" or "Japanese Americans," but it was quickly applied to them. More than five thousand San Franciscans, three thousand of them American citizens, were among those sent to internment camps. Small numbers of German and Italian aliens and a few naturalized citizens were also relocated away from sensitive military installations and some were interned. For almost a year, federal authorities prohibited Italian aliens from leaving port in their fishing boats, injuring San Francisco's fishing industry.

Shipyards around the Bay Area expanded their facilities, and new shipyards were constructed almost overnight to meet the demand for cargo ships. The shipyards were open seven days a week, twenty-four hours a day. Application of assembly-line construction techniques cut production time from 250 days per ship to an average of 25 days. The Bay Area became the country's premier shipbuilding center, producing over one-quarter of the nation's new ships. All this produced a huge demand for workers—more than 260,000. Some new workers were local, including many women who had not done such work before. Others were recruited across the country, including significant numbers from the South, both white and Black.

San Francisco's Black community grew rapidly as migrants, many from the South, came to fill jobs in the shipyards, on the docks, and elsewhere in the booming economy. Many moved into housing in the Western Addition that had recently been vacated by Japanese. Others found housing in Hunters Point, near the shipyards in that area. At the end of the war, in August 1945, a special Census Bureau study found that San Francisco's population was 827,400, an increase of 30 percent from April 1940, including 59,743 military personnel living off base. The Black population had increased by 560 percent, from 4,846 to 32,001. The population of "other races" (those not white or Black) declined by 15 percent, a decline roughly equal to the number of Japanese residents who had been interned.

San Francisco and other cities around the Bay experienced a serious housing shortage, leading some homeowners to create apartments in their basements or attics. The wartime boom in employment put heavy pressure on the Municipal Railway to carry workers to their jobs, but it also created a large surplus in the Muni's budget, large enough to buy all the remaining privately owned streetcar lines and consolidate them into the Muni system.

Most shipyards had contracts with the International Brotherhood of Boilermakers, AFL, which limited membership to whites. Workers at Marinship, in Marin County just north of the Golden Gate Bridge, were represented by Boilermakers Local 6, a long-established local in San Francisco. Faced with many Black workers in the Bay Area shipyards, the Boilermakers Union required them to pay dues to an auxiliary but denied them participation in elections or meetings. Joseph James, a San Franciscan, organized and led the San Francisco Committee Against Discrimination and Segregation, which voted unanimously not to join the auxiliaries. In response, they lost their jobs. After their attorneys secured a temporary restraining order against the layoffs, the National Association for the Advancement of Colored People sent its chief counsel, Thurgood Marshall, to join the lawsuit. In 1944, in *James v. Marinship*, the California Supreme Court unanimously decided for the shipyard workers. By then, however, the shipyards were beginning to close, as the war was entering its final stages.

V-E Day, the end of the war in Europe, came on May 8, 1945, amid momentous events in San Francisco. Between April 25 and June 26, the city hosted the founding conference of the United Nations. Six thousand delegates, staff members, and media representatives crowded hotels and streetcars. The main sessions were held in the Opera House and Veterans' Building. In addition to formal meetings, the Bay Area hosted numerous social events and receptions for the various delegations. As the United Nations' leaders debated a permanent location for its headquarters, the Presidio of San Francisco was given serious

Figure 7.4. Joseph James, in the center wearing dark glasses, is shown in this photo confronting officers of the Boilermakers Union outside their office, as a police officer looks on. Photo courtesy the Sausalito Historical Society.

consideration. Both President Harry Truman and the army agreed, but the Soviet Union refused to consider any West Coast location.

V-J Day, the end of the war with Japan, came on August 14, 1945. The news set off a great celebration. The next day, a celebration on Market Street turned into a riot, mostly by drunken soldiers and sailors who lit bonfires in the street, smashed store windows, attacked and raped women, and disabled thirty streetcars. By the time city police and military police cleared Market Street that night, eleven people were dead and a thousand injured. It was the city's deadliest riot.

City officials tried to ignore the riot and instead to look to a future of international peace when San Francisco would shake off the last vestiges of the Great Depression, when its port would again be the center of commerce on the Pacific Coast, and when the building boom of the 1920s—so long interrupted by depression and war—might resume.

8

Transformations, Turbulence, and Tragedy, 1945–80

The years after World War II brought significant change for San Franciscans, including an economic boom and far-reaching plans to remake much of the city—but some of those plans ran up against stiff opposition. The city's population shifted from 95 percent white in 1940 to 53 percent white by 1980. Racial and ethnic diversity enriched the city's culture but aggravated some social tensions. The new technology of television seemed to be breeding a generation devoted to consumerism and traditional values and gender roles. However, some San Franciscans rebelled, first in the smoky coffeehouses of North Beach, then in largely Black Hunters Point neighborhood, and next in the Haight-Ashbury neighborhood. Turbulence in the 1960s was followed by tragedy in the 1970s.

The New Racial and Ethnic Diversity

The changes in the city's demography that began with an influx of Black workers and their families during World War II continued into the postwar period. A wartime reform of immigration law permitted some immigration from China. Newcomers from Mexico and Central America had been a constant throughout the late nineteenth and early twentieth centuries, and their numbers increased significantly after World War II. In 1965, a major revision of federal immigration law led to increased immigration more generally.

Figure 8.1 indicates the categories used by the Census Bureau to describe the major groups living in the city in 1980.

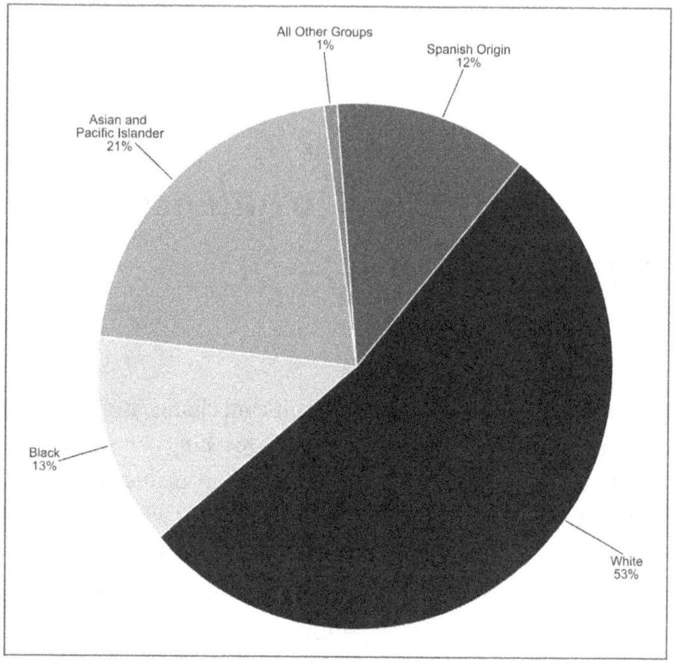

Figure 8.1. San Francisco ethnicity and race based on 1980 census data.

From the time of the Gold Rush until World War II, the city's population had been almost entirely white with small numbers of Chinese and much smaller numbers of African Americans. Throughout those years, census takers reported Latinos as white, so there is no data on the number of San Franciscans of Latino ancestry other than the census reports of the numbers born in Latin America. The 1950 census reported that 3 percent of the city's white population were of Latin American stock (immigrants and the children of immigrants).

The influx of Black families during the war began a transformation of the Western Addition into a largely Black neighborhood by the mid-1960s. Sometimes called the Harlem of the West at that time, the area included Black businesses and entertainment, especially jazz clubs. Though jazz clubs existed elsewhere in the city, they were most numerous along Fillmore Street, an area often called "the Fillmore."

The arrival of large numbers of Black families to San Francisco during the war brought a new focus on civil rights, especially regarding

Figure 8.2. Steve Jackson Jr. created an extensive photo archive documenting the Fillmore and the city's jazz scene more generally. This photo from the early 1950s is of John Handy, Pony Poindexter, John Coltrane, and Frank Fisher at Jimbo's Bop City, the best known of the jazz venues. Photo from the Steve Jackson, Jr., photograph archive, BANC PIC 2022.084, the Bancroft Library, University of California, Berkeley, courtesy Pamela Jackson.

access to housing and jobs. In response, in 1942, prominent Black, Catholic, and Jewish civic leaders formed the Bay Area Council against Discrimination, which became the Council for Civic Unity (CCU) in 1944. The CCU was a significant factor in addressing racial discrimination during the postwar years.

In 1958, major league baseball came to San Francisco when the former New York Giants became the San Francisco Giants. Most San Franciscans celebrated the new team, but Willie Mays, one of the Giants' biggest stars, found that he and his family were not welcome in an upper-middle-class, white neighborhood near St. Francis Wood. Seeking to buy a house there, Mays offered the owner the full asking price. However, nearby homeowners and real estate agents pressured the owner to refuse to sell because of the Mays family's race. The matter immediately became front-page news. Mayor George Christopher gave strong support to Mays, but it was Ed Howden, director of the CCU, who apparently persuaded the seller to accept Mays's offer. Nonetheless, the Mays family never felt welcome in that neighborhood and soon left.

Though not an issue in the Mays situation, many deeds to homes in exclusive neighborhoods had once contained restrictive covenants limiting ownership to whites. The US Supreme Court had ruled such provisions unconstitutional in 1948, but, as the Mays case indicates, that did not end racial discrimination in the sale or rental of real estate. In 1963, a state law prohibited racial discrimination in real estate sales, but the law was overturned by a statewide referendum vote in 1964. However, federal legislation in 1968 barred racial or ethnic discrimination in the sale or rental of housing.

In 1875, the San Francisco school board had closed its separate Black school and ordered that Black students be enrolled in their neighborhood schools. By the early twentieth century, Chinese students had also been admitted to neighborhood schools, but residential patterns meant that the student body of the public school in Chinatown remained entirely Chinese. The California legislature in 1947 prohibited school segregation based on local ordinance, but neighborhood residential patterns produced similar results. As of 1964, some San Francisco schools were more than 90 percent white, others more than 90 percent Black. The Chinatown school remained entirely Chinese, and some schools in the Mission District had a majority of Latino students. In 1971, the federal district court ordered the San Francisco school district to desegregate the schools by bussing students from their neighborhoods. In 1973, the US Supreme Court further complicated San Francisco's school situation by ordering bilingual education for students whose first language was not English; the schools that offered such instruction became disproportionately Chinese. Some white parents voted with their feet. In the mid-1960s, there were more than forty thousand white students in the city's public-school system; by 1980, there were about ten thousand, a decline due only in part to the passing of the postwar "baby boom" through the schools in the 1960s. The issue of equity in public education has continued to be a flash point in the city's politics.

San Francisco in the 1950s

For most San Franciscans, as well as most Americans, the end of World War II came as a great relief. Many, though certainly not all, sought to return to familiar patterns of family life: men as breadwinners, women as homemakers. Television—a new and highly popular technology—featured comedies and dramas that emphasized traditional gender roles. David Riesman, a prominent sociologist, described most Americans in the 1950s as "other-directed," meaning that they sought to fit into societal expectations. Much of the new residential construction in the city fit those expectations: single-family homes where children could walk to public or parochial schools, mothers could shop at neighborhood grocery stores, and fathers could commute downtown to work.

Not all embraced those expectations. San Francisco had always nurtured a bohemian subculture. In the 1920s and 1930s, the area around Montgomery and Washington Streets was the center of the city's arts community, home to artists and writers, who could find cheap food and wine—even during Prohibition—in the Italian cafes of North Beach.

By the 1950s, North Beach coffeehouses and art galleries were offering poetry readings, sometimes accompanied by jazz. In 1950, Lawrence Ferlinghetti and Peter Martin founded City Lights, the first all-paperback bookstore, and two years later launched City Lights Books, publishing the poetry and writings of those sometimes referred to as the San Francisco Renaissance. Jack Kerouac, however, labeled himself and his contemporaries "the Beat Generation." Someone in San Francisco, probably the columnist Herb Caen, turned that into "beatnik," a term disdained by those it was intended to describe. In 1955, at the Six Gallery in North Beach, Allen Ginsberg read his poem, "Howl." The poem indicted materialism, conformity, and the military for destroying the human spirit. Ginsberg, who was gay, used language that some considered obscene. After City Lights published "Howl" in 1956, police arrested Ferlinghetti for distributing obscene material. After a long trial, the judge pronounced that "Howl" was not obscene.

Figure 8.3. City Lights Books, late 1950s. Ferlinghetti is in the upper window, part of the gallery. Photo courtesy City Lights Books.

Growth and Its Discontents, 1945–70

At the end of World War II, San Francisco still held the headquarters of some of the most significant regional corporations, including the Bank of America, Wells Fargo Bank, Crocker Bank, Pacific Gas and Electric, Pacific Telephone, the Southern Pacific railway, and major transpacific shipping lines. The port and manufacturing continued to be major elements in the city's economy. However, the Great Depression and the war had imposed a fifteen-year-long hiatus on private investment in the built environment. At the end of the war, both public agencies and business leaders began to plan major developments.

When the war ended, construction began, expanding residential areas to the west and south, filling nearly all areas still empty, mostly with single-family rowhouses. New office buildings sprouted in the central business district, including the Crown Zellerbach headquarters in 1959, the city's first skyscraper in the then-new International style. Some older downtown buildings got facelifts.

Civic and business leaders initiated large-scale planning. Proposals to transform the city's transportation systems included both a regional rail system and major freeway construction. In 1948, the city created the San Francisco Redevelopment Agency to convert "blighted" areas with new construction, often high-rise buildings. By the 1960s, however, some San Franciscans had begun to question and then to seek limits on such transformative plans.

Late in World War II, the Municipal Railway purchased the last privately owned streetcar lines, but both the rolling stock and the rails on those lines needed major repairs or complete replacements. Most of those streetcar lines were converted to new electric buses, using the existing overhead electric wires. Some lines were simply abandoned. In 1947, Mayor Roger Lapham proposed that the cable-car system should also be dismantled, but a coalition of women's organizations launched an effort to amend the city charter to protect the cable cars. San Francisco voters approved by a margin of more than 3 to 1. The cable cars have continued to run, usually filled with tourists.

Business and civic leaders on both sides of the Bay began to plan new trans-bay transportation to alleviate the congestion clogging the Bay Bridge. From those discussions emerged the San Francisco Bay Area Rapid Transit (BART) Commission, created by the state legislature in 1951. That commission produced a plan for a multicounty rapid-transit district that the state legislature approved in 1957. In 1962, voters in three counties—San Francisco, Alameda (Oakland and Berkeley), and Contra Costa (north and east of Alameda)—approved a bond issue to begin construction, including a tube under the Bay connecting San Francisco and Oakland. The trans-bay tube opened in 1974. One part of the project including putting both BART and Muni tracks under Market Street, freeing the street for motor vehicles. BART has continued to build extensions, including lines into San Mateo and Santa Clara Counties.

Despite such mass transit projects, many planners in the 1950s still considered the automobile the most significant form of transportation, both then and for the future. Because many San Francisco streets had been designed for streetcars and horses, city and state planners sought to redesign the city to accommodate more automobiles. In the late 1950s, in planning a new stadium for the Giants and the San Francisco 49ers (the professional football team), city officials chose

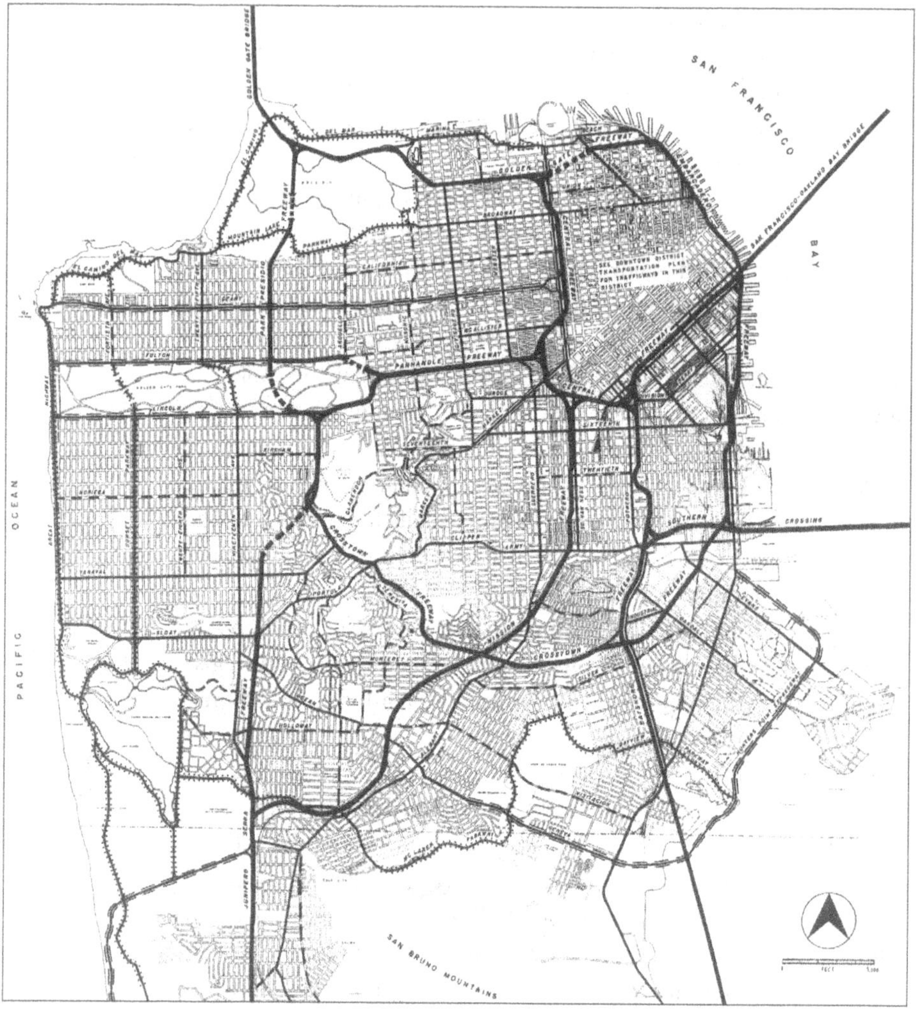

Map 8.1. This is the 1955 version of the various proposals for freeways. On this map, the freeways are the heavy black lines with tunnels designated as dotted heavy black lines. San Francisco Trafficways Plan courtesy Wikimedia Commons.

a site near a freeway that could include ten thousand parking places. City and state agencies were also planning for freeways to crisscross nearly every San Francisco neighborhood except the wealthiest ones. Freeway plans evolved from the late 1940s to the late 1950s, but all

Figure 8.4. The new Southern Freeway, I-280, and the new Glen Park BART station, late 1960s. Aerial photo from *The Bay Area Rapid Transit District Annual Report 1969–1970*, courtesy the Internet Archive.

included one entering near the southwestern corner of the city and moving diagonally toward the waterfront, another running south from the central business district, a third crossing the western part of the city from the southern boundary to the Golden Gate Bridge, and another running west from the central business district, connecting to the western freeway, including converting part of Golden Gate Park to a freeway. Other streets were to be redesigned as multilane expressways with higher speed limits.

By the late 1950s, there was growing hostility to further freeway construction—the beginnings of the city's "Freeway Revolt." Initial construction had disrupted some middle-class and working-class neighborhoods in the southeastern part of the city, but other parts of it had run along old rail lines or through or over industrial districts or the Embarcadero. The next phases of construction targeted middle-class and even a few upper-income neighborhoods. Freeway opponents presented the Board of Supervisors with thirty thousand signatures on a petition calling for an end to freeway construction, and in 1959 the supervisors voted to cancel most freeways still in the planning stage. But freeway proponents didn't give up. New plans were drawn, and the battle continued until 1966, when the supervisors again voted down plans for new freeways. Those under construction at that time stopped in midair.

A similar revolt stopped some plans of the city's Redevelopment Agency (SFRA). One of its early projects was redevelopment of what is now Diamond Heights, then an old rock quarry, barren hilltops, and scattered working-class housing. The SFRA redeveloped the area into a mix of moderate-income and market-rate housing and a small shopping mall, a project completed in 1978. Beginning in the late 1950s, the agency undertook the Golden Gateway project, replacing the old produce market across from the Ferry Building with high-rise buildings, including offices, retail, apartments, and a hotel—a project completed in 1985.

Two other large SFRA projects, one in the South of Market area and the other in the Western Addition, generated such controversy and opposition that both stalled for many years and were ultimately significantly revised before being declared complete.

San Francisco business leaders hoped to redevelop the South of Market area (now called SoMa) and make it an extension of the central business district. That area had long been known as San Francisco's "Skid Row," an area with cheap, single-room lodgings and inexpensive cafes and bars, home to many single men who worked on the waterfront or in other blue-collar jobs or who were seasonal workers outside the city. During the early 1930s, the Communist-led Unemployment Council had launched demonstrations there.

When demolition began, residents organized. Like others in the area, George Woolf was a veteran of the labor organizing of the 1930s.

He and others formed the Tenants and Owners in Opposition to Redevelopment (TOOR). One participant, not surprisingly, described TOOR meetings as "like an old union meeting." TOOR worked closely with lawyers from Neighborhood Legal Assistance and insisted that the Redevelopment Agency must first provide housing before further demolition. In 1970, in a decision with national implications, United States District Judge Stanley Weigel ordered that evictions and demolitions be stopped until the city could provide affordable housing for the people being displaced. The project ground to a halt after two city blocks had been razed.

Redevelopment in the Western Addition also encountered opposition. That project involved a larger area, centered on the Fillmore neighborhood with its high proportion of Black families. There most housing dated to the late nineteenth century. By the 1920s and 1930s, many one- or two-unit buildings had been subdivided into smaller apartments, and that process accelerated during and after World War II. After the area's Japanese population was removed in 1942, the neighborhood became a center of the Black community. In 1948, the Board of Supervisors labeled it "blighted" and endorsed redevelopment plans.

The SFRA divided the Western Addition into two projects, A-1 and A-2. A-1 was centered along Geary Street, which was to be converted into a high-speed expressway. The population of the A-1 was to be reduced by almost 40 percent. Nearly all existing residential buildings were razed. Of the new housing, only a third was for low- and moderate-income families. In their places arose a new Catholic cathedral, several high-rise apartment buildings, a senior living facility, a new post office, and the Japanese Cultural and Trade Center.

Though initial stages of redevelopment created mostly high-rise, market-rate housing, redevelopment plans included an area of low-rise garden apartments. The Redevelopment Agency suggested that the International Longshore and Warehouse Union undertake that project. Convinced that redevelopment had primarily benefited developers, ILWU leaders proposed a housing cooperative for people of low and moderate income: St. Francis Square, at the intersection of Geary and Laguna. St. Francis Square opened in 1963 with 299 apartments in twelve three-story buildings around landscaped courtyards. In

1970, the American Institute of Architects cited the project for "distinguished accomplishment in low- and moderate-income housing." Throughout its existence, St. Francis Square has housed a racially diverse community. But St. Francis Square was the exception in A-1.

When demolition began in A-2, the large area to the south of A-1, more and more families were displaced. In 1963 James Baldwin, a prominent Black novelist, toured the site and famously observed, "urban renewal is Negro removal." The motives of those who planned the project cannot be reduced solely to white racism, but the result was indeed "Negro removal." Like the old Reds in the South of Market area, veterans of ILWU organizing were among those who formed the Western Addition Community Organization (WACO) to oppose further demolition. WACO won a major court decision in 1967, temporarily stopping further work until the SFRA could find suitable housing for those displaced. Nonetheless, by 1970, some 2,500 buildings had been demolished. Eventually St. Francis Square became a model for the development of a few parts of the devastated area. Other parts remained fields of rubble for years. SFRA plans for Chinatown and the Mission District were dropped before they began.

Figure 8.5. The razed city blocks in the center of this photo constituted Redevelopment Area A-2, ca. 1970. The light-colored buildings and the Geary Expressway along the left side were parts of A-1. Photo AAZ-0828 courtesy San Francisco History Center, S.F. Public Library.

While low- and moderate-income residents were fighting the Redevelopment Agency, some upper-income San Franciscans were organizing to oppose what came to be called Manhattanization—the construction of high-rise buildings. Opposition first emerged over a building that blocked the view of the Bay from the upper-income neighborhoods on Russian Hill. In 1964, the Board of Supervisors unanimously approved a height limit along the waterfront north of the Bay Bridge: new construction in low-lying areas was limited to three to four stories, but taller buildings were allowed on the hills.

In the 1970s, Alvin Duskin emerged as the leading spokesman for efforts to restrict high-rise developments more generally. A native San Franciscan who had a successful business designing and selling women's clothing, he was also a social activist. Calling downtown skyscrapers "tombstones," he led unsuccessful ballot initiatives to limit new construction to six stories. But city officials did impose height restrictions in residential areas.

By the 1970s, much of the port was also becoming subject to redevelopment. Beginning in the late 1950s, ocean shipping had moved quickly to the new technology of large containers that were loaded and unloaded by giant cranes. Older freighters quickly became obsolete, as did San Francisco's finger piers. Unlike the Port of San Francisco, the Port of Oakland had space to adjust to containerized shipping and also had more direct access to direct rail and highway links. By 1968, an analysis proposed that much of San Francisco's port be redeveloped as public open spaces, housing, or recreation. After early proposals for high-rise developments were blocked in 1971, subsequent redevelopment of the port proceeded slowly.

San Francisco in the 1960s

The Beat Generation decried conformity but mostly limited its protests to writing and art. In the 1960s, others took a more direct approach to protesting. Movements for Black civil rights were initially focused in the South but soon sparked similar movements elsewhere and among other marginalized groups. Beginning in 1965, all across the country, hundreds and then thousands mobilized in opposition to US military actions in Vietnam. The decade also saw the beginnings of women's and gay and lesbian liberation movements. In the midst of all that, a youth-oriented counterculture emerged amid flowers and hallucinogenic drugs. All had counterparts in San Francisco, which was sometimes at their center. The decade ended with students and faculty of San Francisco State going on strike, American Indians occupying Alcatraz Island, and the first observance of Earth Day.

The tumultuous 1960s began with a forceful confrontation between students and police at San Francisco City Hall. Throughout the 1950s, the Un-American Activities Committee of the US House of Representatives (HUAC) had staged subcommittee hearings across the country, including San Francisco, intended to focus the local media on dramatic charges that a few local residents were part of "the Communist conspiracy." HUAC's tactics drew increasing criticism from civil liberties advocates.

HUAC announced three days of subcommittee hearings in May 1960, to be held in the Supervisors' Chambers of City Hall. HUAC's critics organized, mobilizing students from San Francisco State College; the University of California, Berkeley; and other Bay Area schools. HUAC announced the hearings as open to the public, but committee staff issued enough passes to its supporters to fill nearly all the seats. On the first day of the hearings, a thousand protestors marched to City Hall where they were told the Supervisors' Chambers were already full. On the next day, throngs of students were again left outside. They began singing and shouting to be admitted and refused to disperse. Police turned a firehose on the demonstrators, soaking them and cascading water down the wide, marble steps from the second floor to the first floor. Helmeted police clubbed demonstrators and dragged them down the wet steps and outside into waiting paddy wagons. Sixty-four were arrested, but all charges were quickly dismissed. Soon after, Mayor George Christopher announced that HUAC was no longer allowed to use city buildings. For many in the Bay Area, especially students, the "City Hall swim" marked the beginning of two decades of protests and demonstrations.

Soon after, inspired by civil rights activism in the South in the late 1950s and 1960s, Black San Franciscans, especially young people, began to target employers who discriminated against Black job candidates.

In 1963, they demonstrated at Mel's Drive-In, then in 1964 at the Palace Hotel. The largest demonstrations, also in 1964, were at the auto showrooms that then lined several blocks of Van Ness Avenue. The demonstrators included members of all races, including white students from San Francisco State and UC Berkeley. Thousands sat down in auto showrooms and blocked part of Van Ness. More than two hundred were arrested. In the end, the auto companies signed an agreement not to discriminate. A young Black lawyer, Willie Brown, represented some of the demonstrators.

Elsewhere in the country, the 1960s saw some of the most widespread and violent rioting in the nation's history, many of which began as Black residents of inner cities protested against police violence and then rioted by attacking police, news people, and local stores. In 1966, San Francisco experienced its only such riot, after police shot and killed a Black teenager fleeing from a stolen car in Hunters Point, a neighborhood of deteriorating housing dating to World War II that had been slated for redevelopment and from which some residents were being evicted. The governor mobilized the National Guard and imposed martial law for several days.

Beginning in 1965, protests were also aimed at the growing US military presence in Vietnam. In April 1967, fifty thousand to sixty thousand antiwar marchers in San Francisco walked from downtown to an antiwar rally in Golden Gate Park, and similar marches became annual events for the duration of the war. In addition, some activists sought to block military facilities or counseled young men facing the draft.

A very different, and much gentler, protest against mainstream culture began in the Haight-Ashbury neighborhood, a commercial and residential area built up in the 1890s and early 1900s. The cheap rents and large rooms of the old houses and flats attracted young people. Some focused on creatively reimagining society, seeking alternative social and ecological systems, creating a counterculture based on sharing rather than acquisition, and living with nature rather than harnessing it. By 1963, some were calling these young people hippies, a modification of the term "hipster" that some of the Beat Generation had preferred. Like the Beats, hippies were interested in sexual freedom (made easier for women by oral contraceptives, first available in

1960), non-Western religious experiences, and mind-altering drugs. Where the Beats had enjoyed marijuana, hippies added psychedelics, especially LSD (lysergic acid diethylamide, often called simply "acid"), promoted by Timothy Leary, a former Harvard psychologist, and Ken Kesey, who had first encountered LSD in tests by the CIA at a veterans' hospital. By the mid-1960s, young people attracted by the hippie lifestyle were descending on the Haight-Ashbury district and nearby parts of Golden Gate Park. By then, acid was widely available in the Haight.

By the mid-1960s, local bands, notably Jefferson Airplane, the Grateful Dead, and Big Brother and the Holding Company, were producing music that soon came to be called the San Francisco Sound. In January 1966, Kesey, events-organizer Bill Graham, and several others rented the new ILWU hall in North Beach for a three-day Trips Festival, advertised as drug-free, although LSD was nonetheless prominent. For three nights, the large hall was filled with light shows and rock bands. Bands also contributed free outdoor concerts. A Love Pageant Rally in October 1966, in the Golden Gate Park Panhandle, near Haight Street, attracted several thousand people to listen to music by the Grateful Dead and by Janis Joplin and her band, Big Brother and the Holding Company. Such events attracted national celebrities. Joan Baez, the folk singer, played her guitar and sang on Haight Street. George Harrison of the Beatles joined a crowd in Golden Gate Park. In January 1967, a Human Be-In at Golden Gate Park's Polo Field attracted some thirty thousand to thirty-five thousand people. Those who attended heard from Leary, Ginsberg, other Beat figures, radicals, and peace activists. Several bands performed, including the Grateful Dead. Ralph Gleason, music critic for the *San Francisco Chronicle*, described it as an "affirmation, not a protest . . . a promise of good, not evil . . . something truly new."

The vibrant music scene of the mid-1960s produced a number of bands, including two that broke previous racial and gender patterns. Sly and the Family Stone, led by Sly Stone, included both Black and white band members at a time when nearly all bands were of the same ethnicity. At a time when women were largely limited to being vocalists, the Family Stone included women who played instruments as well as sang. Santana, the band led by and named for Carlos Santana, who was born and grew up in Mexico, fused rock with Latin American jazz; like the Family Stone, Santana included members of various ethnicities.

Media coverage of the outdoor concerts and the Human Be-In stoked national interest in the Haight-Ashbury scene. In the spring of 1967, young people across the country were singing that, if they were going to San Francisco, they should be sure to wear flowers in their hair. San Francisco groups associated with the hippies and local churches began to anticipate that thousands of young people might come to the city that summer for what the media was hyping as the Summer of Love. In response, the city officials futilely announced

GRACE SLICK COMPOSES "WHITE RABBIT," 1965–66

Grace Slick became the lead singer for Jefferson Airplane in 1966. She had previously held that place in another band, the Great Society. Among the songs she brought to Jefferson Airplane was "White Rabbit," which has been called "the cornerstone of psychedelic rock" and "an LSD drenched classic." In 2011, the *Wall Street Journal* claimed that Slick's singing "ignited a psychedelic-rock revolution that put San Francisco on the map."

Slick later explained that she'd written "White Rabbit" in late 1965 or early 1966 while on an acid trip—LSD was then legal and widely available in San Francisco. The song draws heavily on Lewis Carroll's books, *Alice in Wonderland* and *Through the Looking Glass*, which were among Slick's childhood favorites. She later said, "Alice was on her own, and she was in a very strange place, but she kept on going and she followed her curiosity—that's the White Rabbit." Slick added, "The 1960s resembled Wonderland for me. Like Alice, I met all kinds of strange characters, but I was comfortable with it." She also acknowledged, "The song is a little dark. It's not saying everything's going to be wonderful. The Red Queen is shouting 'off with her head' and the 'White Knight is talking backwards.'"

Slick first wrote the lyrics, then composed the music: "I wrote 'White Rabbit' on a red upright piano that cost me about $50. It had eight or 10 keys missing, but that was OK because I could hear in my head the notes that weren't there." She'd recently been listening to Miles Davis's jazz version of Ravel's *Bolero*, and she gave 'White Rabbit' a similar driving rhythm that builds to a crescendo that she later likened to an orgasm.

Years later, Slick observed, "Writing weird stuff about Alice backed by a dark Spanish march was in step with what was going on in San Francisco then. We were all trying to get as far away from the expected as possible."

that hippies were "unwelcome." Some seventy-five thousand young people descended on the Haight that summer.

A group of concerned medical professionals opened the Haight Ashbury Free Clinic in early June 1967 to provide counseling, education, and medical care. They treated twelve thousand patients in the first month for drug issues, venereal disease, infections, pneumonia, and malnourishment. Huckleberry House opened to provide young people who were "runaways" with temporary shelter, medical assistance, and counseling. The Diggers (an anarchist commune), other community organizations, and individuals contributed to assisting those who arrived with no place to live and little money for food and shelter. Many nonetheless ended up living on the streets, sleeping where they could find a place, and panhandling for money for food and drugs.

The throngs of idealistic and naive young people attracted predators of various sorts, including drug dealers and petty criminals. Crime became so rampant along Haight Street that many of the local businesses closed. The Haight became a site of drug addiction and related problems as methamphetamines and heroin replaced LSD and marijuana as the dominant drugs. Deaths from heroin overdoses multiplied, including one of the decade's most prominent vocalists, Janis Joplin, in 1970.

In December 1969, thousands of hippies and other San Franciscans traveled across the Bay to Altamont, southeast of Oakland, for a Rolling Stones concert. The band hired members of the Hell's Angels motorcycle gang to provide security, but the gang members terrorized and assaulted the audience, and stabbed one young man to death. Three others also died. Altamont became the symbolic end of what had reached its high point with the Summer of Love.

The most complete reporting on the Altamont disaster came from *Rolling Stone* magazine. Founded in San Francisco in 1967, it focused on rock music, found a large audience, and helped make the Bay Area a global rock capital. Both a product of the San Francisco counterculture and one of its shrewdest observers, *Rolling Stone* mixed music journalism with political commentary and investigative reporting. It received a national award for its Altamont coverage and remained in San Francisco until 1977, when it moved to New York. It has been described as the journalistic voice of its generation.

By 1968, protests were taking place worldwide, for differing causes in different places. In the US, there were protests over the war in Vietnam, in support of women's liberation, and, on college campuses, in support of expanding the rights of students. At San Francisco State College (now University), a student strike lasted for five months and brought a faculty strike in its wake, the longest such strike in US higher education. Student strike demands initially focused on changes in admission policies and on student control of some curriculum and hiring. When student strike leaders tried to shut down classes and occupy buildings (as had happened the previous spring at Columbia University), intervention by city police led to violent clashes. Faculty members, alarmed by the growing violence, voted to strike, hoping their action would stop the police violence. The strikes finally ended in March 1969 with agreements that included the creation of the Black Studies Department within the School of Ethnic Studies.

The strike at San Francisco State provides one example of how the civil rights movement among Black Americans in the 1950s and 1960s encouraged other movements for rights and liberation, including movements by Asian Americans, Indigenous Americans, and Latinos. The new School of Ethnic Studies at San Francisco State included departments of American Indian Studies, Asian American Studies, Black Studies, and La Raza (Latina/o) Studies.

In 1969, a group calling themselves the United Indians of All Tribes, including students from San Francisco State, occupied Alcatraz Island. The island was then empty. From 1933 to 1963, it had been a high-security federal prison. The prison closed in 1963, and the island became surplus federal property. San Francisco had a significant population of Indigenous Americans from around the country who had relocated to the city as part of the Bureau of Indian Affairs policy of terminating reservations. The United Indians of All Tribes claimed the island under a treaty provision from 1868 that promised to return abandoned federal property to the Indigenous people from whom it had been taken. Red Power activists from around the country came to join the initial occupying group. The occupation lasted nearly two years. During the occupation, President Richard Nixon ended the termination policy and initiated a new federal policy based on self-determination for reservation residents. After the occupying group left, the National Park Service incorporated Alcatraz into the Golden Gate National Recreation Area and now offers educational tours and exhibitions of the history of the island, including the prison and the occupation.

The Zodiac and Zebra Murders

In the late 1960s, a mysterious serial killer self-identified as Zodiac taunted the police with letters, some in code, to Bay Area newspapers. Zodiac is known to have killed five people and seriously wounded two others, one in San Francisco and the rest in the Bay Area. Zodiac's letters to newspapers claimed to have killed many more, including in Southern California. Zodiac's last letter was in 1974. The murders have never been solved.

Another wave of serial murders began in late 1973. Between October 20, 1973, and April 16, 1974, fifteen people were murdered and eight seriously injured. The victims were white, and the assailants were Black. San Francisco police used their Z (Zebra) radio frequency in their manhunt for the murderers, and the events became known as the Zebra murders. By January, the murders were creating a panic as people avoided being on the streets. In late April, an informant came forward, leading to the conviction of four Black men, who were sentenced to life in prison. Among the victims who survived was Art Agnos, who later became mayor.

Gender Liberation Movements

The civil rights movements of the 1950s and 1960s led to similar movements for the rights of women and of gays and lesbians. A women's movement emerged in the 1960s, called second-wave feminism (to distinguish it from the first wave in the late nineteenth and early twentieth centuries). In San Francisco, women who had been involved with the civil rights and antiwar movements began to organize around a wide range of women's issues. Women opened feminist bookstores. College faculty members developed Women's Studies courses at local

Figure 8.6. After buying their own building in 1979, the San Francisco Women's Centers initiated a major mural project in the 1990s, creating *MaestraPeace* (Woman Teacher of Peace), covering two sides of the Women's Building and reaching five stories high. Photo courtesy MAESTRAPEACE Mural, ©1994 and 2000, Juana Alicia Miranda Bergman, Edythe Boone, Susan Kelk Cervantes, Meera Desai, Yvonne Littleton, and Irene Perez, All Rights Reserved.

colleges and universities, including San Francisco State, one of the first. In 1979, the San Francisco Women's Centers purchased a four-story building in the Mission District, originally a German gymnastics club, then a Norwegian social center, which they converted into the nation's first woman-owned and woman-operated community center.

Developing parallel to and sometimes overlapping with the women's movement were movements for gay and lesbian rights. Four lesbian couples in San Francisco formed the Daughters of Bilitis in 1955. (Bilitis was understood to be a contemporary of the Greek poet Sappho, known for her poetry about love between women.) Soon after, a chapter of the Mattachine Society was founded by San Francisco gay men. ("Mattachine" came from a character in Italian theater who was permitted to speak truth to the king.) In 1965, when those organizations joined with other homophile groups to hold a fundraising ball, the police photographed all those who attended and arrested four lawyers who protested the police actions. When twenty-five of the city's leading attorneys joined the four lawyers' defense, the judge directed the jury to bring a verdict of not guilty.

A more violent protest came the next year, in the Tenderloin District, west of the central business district and north of Market Street, an area with cheap apartments or single rooms, where prostitution flourished. The Tenderloin was also home to a number of transgender women and gay men, especially drag queens. Some transgender (now

Figure 8.7. Harvey Milk began campaigning for office in 1973, one year after he moved to San Francisco. As he became more experienced in city politics, he reached out to voters across the political spectrum and secured early support from organized labor. This photo, from June 1977 shows him registering voters outside his camera store. One of his first actions as a supervisor was to secure passage of a city ordinance requiring dog owners to scoop their pets' feces, an issue that had long rankled nearly all San Franciscans. Photo GLC-0022, courtesy San Francisco History Center, San Francisco Public Library.

often called trans) women and drag queens were also sex workers. Trans women and drag queens often gathered late at night at Compton's Cafeteria in the Tenderloin. Police regularly arrested them for female impersonation or cross-dressing. In August 1966, an attempt to arrest one trans woman led to a full-scale riot aimed at the police. Historian Susan Stryker has described the Compton's Cafeteria riot as "the first known incident of collective militant queer resistance to police harassment in U.S. history."

By the 1960s, increasing numbers of gay men were moving to the neighborhood around Castro Street south of Market Street. By the 1970s, the Castro had become known as the largest gay neighborhood in the US, replete with gay bars and other businesses.

In 1972, Harvey Milk moved to San Francisco and opened a camera store on Castro Street. He soon ran for public office, but was unsuccessful in his repeated campaigns. Then, in 1977, when the city for the first time elected supervisors by district rather than at large, Milk won, becoming the first openly gay person to be elected to public office in California.

Change at City Hall

Milk was not the only new face in City Hall. For more than fifty years, beginning with James Rolph's election in 1911, successful businessmen had filled the officially nonpartisan mayor's office. Rolph and his four successors were all Republicans. In 1963, however, change came to City Hall with the election of John F. Shelley as mayor. Shelley, a liberal Democrat, had previously served in the state legislature and the US House of Representatives. Before seeking elective office, he had headed the San Francisco Labor Council. His four-year mayoral term included the Summer of Love, the Hunters Point riot, and the growing opposition to SFRA projects. Shelley appointed the city's first Black supervisor when a vacancy opened on that board. Every mayor since Shelley has been a Democrat.

In 1968, Joseph Alioto succeeded Shelley as mayor. A successful lawyer, known as supportive of the Redevelopment Agency, Alioto was elected with strong support from the city's unions, especially the ILWU. He appointed union members and Blacks to every city commission.

San Francisco's yeasty political mix in the 1960s produced a new generation of city leaders. Sue Bierman entered city politics as part of the Freeway Revolt and continued to address neighborhood issues; Mayor George Moscone appointed her to the planning commission in 1976, and she was elected to the Board of Supervisors in 1992. Dianne Feinstein had entered city politics as a freeway opponent and had campaigned against Manhattanization; she was elected to the Board of Supervisors in 1969 and later became the city's first female mayor and then the state's first female US Senator. In 1964, Willie Brown, who had been active in the civil rights demonstrations and the Western Addition controversy, was elected to the state assembly. He spent thirty years in that body, including fifteen years as speaker.

Willie Brown had met John Burton when they were students at San Francisco State College in the late 1950s. In 1956, John Burton's older brother, Phillip Burton, had won election to the California Assembly. In 1964, Phillip Burton was elected to Congress, the same year that Willie Brown and John Burton were elected to the California State Assembly. The Burton-Brown organization—sometimes called the Burton-Brown machine—became a potent political force, pushing city, state, and national politics to the left. In Congress in 1974, Phillip Burton led the successful effort to abolish HUAC, and in 1976 he narrowly lost a bid to become majority leader. George Moscone, elected to the California senate in 1966, was an important ally. In 1975, Moscone in the senate and Brown in the assembly pushed through AB489, which decriminalized private sex acts between consenting adults, the first such legislation in the nation.

Later that same year, 1975, George Moscone was narrowly elected mayor over John Barbagelata, a conservative supervisor. Moscone had been a supervisor and state senator, including senate majority leader. Allied with Brown and the Burton brothers, Moscone based his campaign on appealing to neighborhood activists, women, LGBT people, and people of color. As mayor, he appointed representatives of those groups to city boards and commissions. In 1977, he and the progressive district attorney and sheriff survived a recall election organized by Barbagelata. Moscone resolved the imbroglio in the South of Market redevelopment area so that construction could begin on the park and the convention center that was later to bear his name.

In 1976, voters had approved an amendment to the city charter changing the method for electing supervisors, from citywide elections to election by districts. That amendment changed the board: after the 1977 election, several neighborhood activists replaced residents of the city's elite neighborhoods. In addition to Harvey Milk, the new supervisors included Gordon Lau, the first Chinese American to serve on the board, and Carol Ruth Silver, who claimed to be the board's first unwed mother.

Tragedy

November 1978 was a month of tragedy for San Francisco. The first took place far away, in the nation of Guyana, on the northeastern coast of South America. That tragedy had its beginnings in 1965, when Jim Jones, an ordained minister, moved his Peoples Temple to San Francisco. Jones preached a fundamentalist version of Protestantism mixed with a strong commitment to equal rights for all races and what he called Apostolic Socialism. Located in the Western Addition, the Peoples Temple quickly attracted a large, predominantly Black congregation. Though Jones's organization became increasingly authoritarian, secretive, and abusive internally, Jones carefully cultivated relations with prominent liberal Democrats. His ability to turn out large numbers of Temple members to mobilize voters made him popular in City Hall. Mayor Moscone appointed Jones to a city commission and helped him to become the presiding officer.

After increasingly critical media accounts of the cultlike aspects of the Peoples Temple, Jones in late 1973 decided to move the congregation to Guyana, a former British colony with a socialist government. Temple members began to build Jonestown in the jungle west of the Guyanese capital, Georgetown. Jones himself moved in late 1977, as investigative reporters were publishing accounts of his authoritarian and abusive practices. By 1978, some nine hundred Temple members were living there. Jones, however, was becoming increasingly paranoid and conducted regular exercises to prepare Temple members for what he called revolutionary suicide.

Given accounts of life in Jonestown, Congressman Leo Ryan, whose district included part of San Francisco, flew to Jonestown on November 17, 1978, along with staff members and reporters. After they met with Jones, some Temple members secretly asked Ryan to take them with him when he left. The next day, as the group prepared to board their planes, Temple security guards opened fire, killing Ryan and several others. One plane managed to take off. That night, Jones led the Temple members to drink poison, and he shot himself. More than nine hundred people died on November 18. The initial accounts reached San Francisco the next day, but the full horror of the mass suicide and murders became known only over the next few days.

As San Franciscans were reeling from the unfolding news from Jonestown, they were further shocked by the assassination of Mayor Moscone and Supervisor Milk on November 27. The assassin was Dan White, who had been elected to the Board of Supervisors at the same time as Milk. White, an Irish Catholic, had been a police officer and then a firefighter. He apparently saw himself as defending traditional values against gays and pot smokers. Unable to make a go of a small business and out of his depth on the board, he resigned as supervisor. He then changed his mind and asked the mayor to reappoint him. Moscone refused.

On November 27, White smuggled a gun into City Hall. He repeatedly shot Moscone, then Milk. He surrendered to police at the station where he had once worked. Dianne Feinstein, president of the Board of Supervisors, automatically became acting mayor, informed the city of the tragedy, and declared a state of mourning.

San Franciscans were stunned, shocked, horrified. That evening, thirty thousand people gathered in the Castro and walked with candles down Market Street to City Hall for an impromptu service of mourning. As speakers were unable to find the right words, Joan Baez was repeatedly called upon to sing, including "Amazing Grace." Lawrence Ferlinghetti composed "An Elegy to Dispel Gloom," but the tumultuous sixties and seventies ended in sadness and dismay.

PORTFOLIO C

San Francisco's Turbulent Sixties

Figure C.1. On May 13, 1960, police turned fire hoses on nonviolent student demonstrators against HUAC, then dragged them down the water-slickened steps inside City Hall and into a waiting police van. Photo AAF-1023 courtesy San Francisco History Center, San Francisco Public Library.

Figure C.2. These picketers outside City Hall, April 18, 1961, were protesting against the Southern Freeway proposal. San Francisco's "freeway revolt" brought together old Reds from the 1930s, society matrons, and middle-class housewives. Photo AAF-067, from *San Francisco News-Call-Bulletin*, courtesy San Francisco History Center, San Francisco Public Library.

Figure C.3. In 1963, civil rights pickets were arrested at Mel's Drive-In, protesting what they called the discriminatory hiring practices of its owner, Harold Dobbs, a candidate for mayor. Protestors then rallied inside City Hall, protesting against both Mel's hiring practices and police brutality. Dobbs lost to John Shelley for mayor. Photo AAK-0878, from *San Francisco News-Call-Bulletin*, courtesy San Francisco History Center, San Francisco Public Library.

Figure C.4. On April 15, 1967, people from around the western US joined San Franciscans—some fifty thousand to sixty thousand in all—to march in the Spring Mobilization against the War in Vietnam. Another 125,000 marched the same day in New York City. Photo by George Garrigues, courtesy Wikimedia Commons.

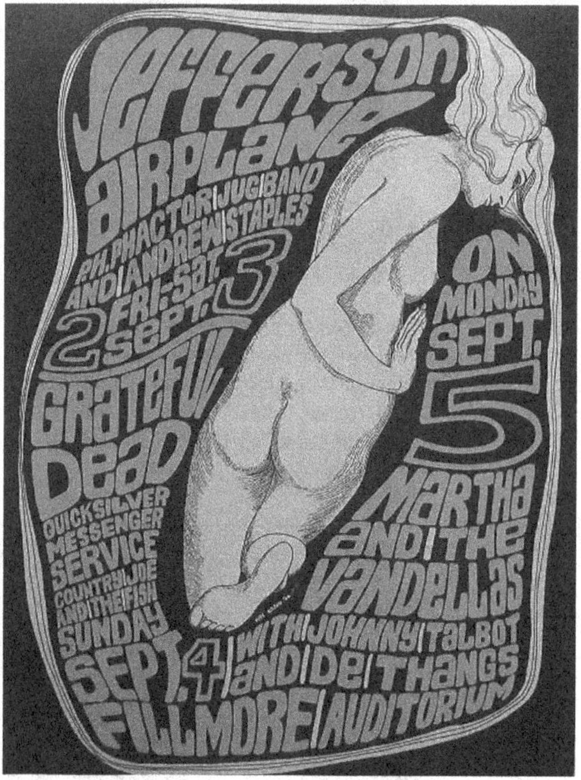

Figure C.5. By the mid-1960s, Bill Graham had emerged as the leading impresario for bands who were creating the San Francisco Sound. The Fillmore Auditorium was the major locale. Wes Wilson created this poster in 1966, announcing several of the city's leading bands. Wilson's distinctive posters helped to define the era. Courtesy of Wes Wilson and FoundSF, Creative Commons.

Figure C.6. The Jefferson Airplane, 1967, posing for Herb Greene in his dining room: back row, Jack Casady, Grace Slick, Marty Balin; front row, Jorma Kaukonen, Paul Kantner, Spencer Dryden. Grace Slick and Janice Joplin, with their distinctive ranges and qualities, were the most memorable vocalists of the San Francisco Sound. In 1999, Joplin was ranked third and Slick was twentieth on VH1's 100 Greatest Women of Rock N Roll. Photo courtesy Herb Greene.

Figure C.7. The Grateful Dead—Jerry Garcia, Ron "Pigpen" McKernan, Phil Lesh, Bob Weir, Bill Kreutzmann—posed for Herb Greene in early 1967 around the street sign marking the intersection of Haight and Ashbury Streets, symbolic center of the 1960s counterculture. The Dead continued to tour and perform until the death of Garcia in 1995, and variations of the group have periodically performed since. In 2004, *Rolling Stone* ranked the Grateful Dead No. 57 on their list of the 100 Greatest Artists of All Time. Photo courtesy Herb Greene.

Figure C.8. (above) Student strikers, San Francisco State College, November 1968. Photo by Tim Drescher, courtesy FoundSF, Creative Commons.

Figure C.9. (right) Alcatraz, November 29, 1969. Courtesy FoundSF, Creative Commons.

9

San Francisco Since 1980

San Francisco continues to experience dramatic changes—changes in the number of people, changes in the ethnic composition of the population, changes in the city's economy and workforce, changes in the built environment. Two epidemics complicated the social, cultural, and economic changes—HIV/AIDS in the 1980s and COVID in the 2020s.

Some have seen parallels between San Francisco's Gilded Age in the late nineteenth century and its history since about 1980. Both saw individuals and corporations develop great wealth and great power, especially through new technologies. Both saw the newly wealthy compete to erect taller and taller buildings. Both saw acute poverty side by side with ostentatious displays of wealth. San Francisco's first Gilded Age ended spectacularly in 1906 amid earthquake and fire. It is not yet clear if San Francisco's second Gilded Age has run its course.

Demographic Changes

After World War II, San Francisco's civilian population fell steadily, from 767,657 in 1945 to 678,974 in 1980. That long-term trend reversed in the 1980s, with the population rising to an all-time high of 874,784 in 2020, then declining to 827,526 in 2024. Those changes reflected changes in the city's economy and were accompanied by changes in ethnic patterns. By the first decades of the twenty-first century, San Francisco had become highly diverse by ethnicity and gender. The 1990 census registered that San Francisco no longer had a majority of whites. Figure 9.1 summarizes the findings of the 2020 census, which confirmed patterns that had been developing over the previous several decades: the city's largest ethnic groups were whites, Asians, and Latinos. The Black population of the city has been steadily declining, both proportionately and in absolute numbers since 1970, when Blacks accounted for 13 percent of the total and 96,078 individuals. The 2020 census counted 42,803 Black residents of San Francisco.

What the graph cannot show is the diversity *within* these groups. The census has consistently shown that the largest single group among Asians has been Chinese, constituting more than 20 percent of the city's population, but Asians have also recently included Vietnamese, Koreans, Japanese, and South Asians, all between 1 and 2 percent. The largest group of Latinos has been Mexicans, with more than 7 percent of the total population; Salvadorans, Nicaraguans, and Guatemalans have accounted for 1–2 percent each. "Other races" includes Indigenous Americans, Pacific Islanders, and those of mixed race. More than a third of the city's residents have been born outside the United States. The largest number of white immigrants have come from the former Soviet Union, especially Ukraine and Russia.

While members of any ethnic group can be found anywhere in the city, there are geographic concentrations of some of groups. Outside

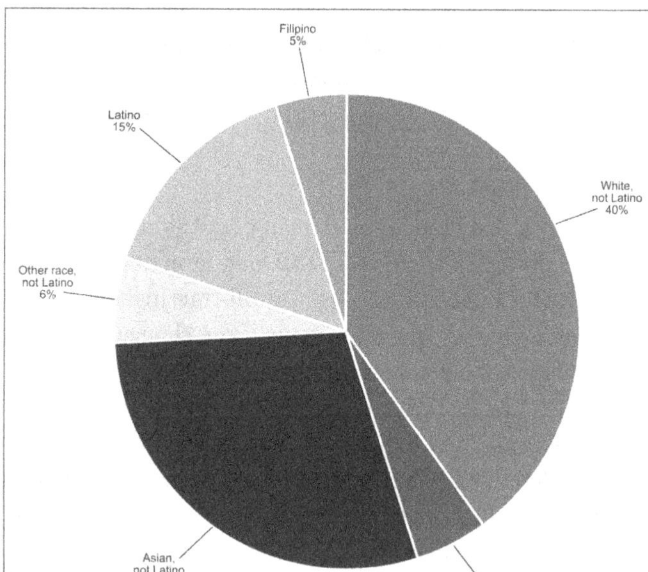

Figure 9.1. San Francisco ethnicity and race based on 2020 census data.

of Chinatown, many of Chinese ancestry live in the western parts of the Richmond and Sunset districts and the southeastern part of the city. Many Filipinos live in the south-central part of the city, near the large concentration of Filipinos in Daly City, comprising together the largest concentration of Filipinos in the US. The largest concentrations of Black people live in the Hunters Point area or the Ingleside neighborhood, with fewer in the Western Addition. Latinos are most likely to live in the Mission District. There, bold, colorful public murals in the style of the 1920s–30s Mexican muralists grace public buildings, private property, and even fences and garage doors.

San Francisco has more gender diversity than most parts of the nation. A recent study indicates that just over 15 percent of San Franciscans identify as LGBT, the highest proportion of any major city. Only 36 percent of the city's households are of married couples. The city also has the lowest proportion of children of any major city.

San Franciscans differs significantly from national averages in other ways. As of 2020, 59 percent of city residents had graduated

Figure 9.2. The Rectory of St. Peter's Church, at 24th and Florida Streets, features these bold and colorful murals depicting the history and struggles of Latino/a peoples. That area is filled with similar murals, often with a political message. Photo by and courtesy Chris Carlsson.

from college (compared to 48 percent nationally), and nearly a quarter had graduate or professional degrees (compared to 14 percent nationally), a reflection of post-1980 economic developments in the city. Only 12 percent ended their schooling at high school, half the national proportion.

San Francisco has long been second to New York as the most densely populated city in the US. Not surprisingly, 62 percent of the city's housing units are rentals. Though the city's population has increased by 38 percent since 1940, the number of housing units has increased by 79 percent—understandable only because the average housing unit in 1940 held three people, and the average housing unit in 2020 held two.

Economic Transformations

Some of the variations in the city's population, especially the higher educational levels, reflect significant changes in the city's economy. In the 1970s, San Francisco was still home to major manufacturing enterprises, most dating to the late nineteenth or early twentieth century. All that changed with surprising quickness. Many sources of blue-collar employment disappeared. Union Iron Works, which had become part of Bethlehem Steel in 1905, closed down in 1980. Schlage Lock, a major manufacturing enterprise since the 1920s, was acquired by Ingersoll-Rand in 1974, moved some operations out of the city in 1976, and closed its large San Francisco complex in 1999. Levi Strauss closed its San Francisco plant in 2002. Smaller manufacturing concerns also closed or moved. Containerization of ocean shipping not only accelerated the movement of manufacturing to locations outside the US but also made the port's finger piers and warehouses obsolete, eliminating many blue-collar jobs for longshore and warehouse workers, teamsters, and railroad workers.

White-collar employment was less affected, but there were important changes. In the 1970s, San Francisco had included major corporate headquarters. The Crown Zellerbach Corporation was acquired in a hostile takeover by a British investor in 1985 and dismantled. The Southern Pacific company was similarly broken up in the 1990s. Crocker Bank was absorbed by Wells Fargo in 1986;

Wells Fargo, in turn, was acquired by a Minnesota bank in 1998, but kept its name, and the merged headquarters remained in San Francisco. The Bank of America was purchased by a North Carolina bank in 1998 and kept its name, but corporate headquarters moved to North Carolina.

These changes did not affect San Francisco's appeal to tourists. Tourism had long been a significant part of the city's economy, but by the 1980s much of the northern waterfront had been transformed from industrial uses to tourism. In the early 1960s, the city block that had once housed the food processing operations of the Ghirardelli Company was converted to a complex of restaurants and retail; much of it now houses an upscale residential hotel. The former Del Monte cannery and warehouse followed a similar path in the mid-1960s. Pier 39, a tourist-oriented complex of restaurants, retail, and entertainment, opened in 1978.

In 1972, through legislation spearheaded by San Francisco's Congressman Phillip Burton in response to advocacy by local residents, federal property around both sides of the Golden Gate became the Golden Gate National Recreation Area (GGNRA), which now attracts seventeen million visitors each year. In 1978, the National Park Service acquired the city's Maritime Museum and its pier, historic ships, and other buildings near the northern end of the waterfront. They became central components the San Francisco Maritime National Historical Park.

When Fort Mason was no longer needed as the army's major port of embarkation to the Pacific, it became part of the GGNRA in the mid-1970s and now houses the Fort Mason Center for Arts and Culture, a significant example of the adaptive reuse of a former military base. When the army declared the Presidio of San Francisco surplus in the early 1990s, developers looked at it greedily, but Burton's 1972 legislation had included it within the GGNRA. However, the Republican Congress in 1996 specified that the Presidio had to be self-supporting and created the Presidio Trust to administer the built environment of the Presidio to make it self-sufficient. The National Park Service's role has been limited to the parts of the Presidio bordering the water and to interpretation.

In the 1980s and 1990s, the San Francisco Bay Area emerged as a major center for computer- and internet-related technology companies. In the 1950s, the silicon transistor was developed south of San Francisco, near Stanford University. Early personal computing companies, notably Apple, were located in what was soon called Silicon Valley, between Stanford and San Jose. The concept of Silicon Valley steadily expanded and came to include San Francisco.

The development of personal computers in the 1970s and the expansion of the internet to ordinary citizens in the 1980s laid the basis for creation of internet-based companies selling goods and services. By 1998, when NASDAQ made it possible to buy and sell stock online, especially stock in the emerging technology companies, San Francisco had become a major center for these new technologies. As technology companies continued to flourish to its south, San Francisco also became a bedroom community for many tech employees. These new industries brought population growth that created a housing shortage that dramatically drove up housing costs.

In the late 1990s, the value of technology companies listed on NASDAQ increased by 800 percent in what was soon called the "dot-com boom." For a time, it seemed that the sky was the limit for computer- and internet-related ventures, and the most amazing varieties of companies launched, some based on little more than an idea and borrowed funds. The stock price of some startups jumped by as much as 400 percent on the first day of offering. However, by 2000 it had become clear that the new industry had expanded beyond consumer demand and the dot-com boom went bust. Many of the new companies closed. Those that survived, however, laid a more substantial basis for future expansion of technology-related companies in the San Francisco Bay Area.

Transformation of SoMa (South of Market Area)

Before his death, Mayor George Moscone had brokered a compromise that permitted construction in the long-stalled Redevelopment Agency's SoMa project. That project was completed in 1981. One city block houses the Moscone Center, a major convention center. Most of the other city block, just south of Mission Street, became a public park,

Yerba Buena Gardens, centered on a dramatic memorial to Martin Luther King Jr. That block also contains the Yerba Buena Center for the Arts on the east side and commercial space on the west. Two nearby apartment buildings for those displaced are named for George Woolf and Robert Mendelsohn, TOOR leaders.

Surrounding areas transformed into an arts and cultural district. The most significant institution anchoring that development was the San Francisco Museum of Modern Art (SFMOMA), which had begun in the 1930s in the upper floors of the Veterans' Building in the Civic Center. In 1995, SFMOMA moved into a dramatic new building, across Third Street from the Yerba Buena Center for the Arts. Other arts and cultural organizations followed, including the Museum of the African Diaspora and the Contemporary Jewish Museum. SFMOMA opened a large addition in 2016. Upscale hotels, restaurants, and bars clustered nearby.

All this was in keeping with the Downtown Plan, a master plan for future downtown development adopted by the Board of Supervisors in 1985. The plan specified that new commercial development should take place primarily in SoMa, integrating much of that area into the central business district. New hotel construction was guided to the area around the Moscone Center. The plan also sought to protect historic buildings and the character of historic districts. Chinatown received special protection, partly to maintain its appeal to tourists.

The HIV/AIDS Epidemic

In July 1981, the Centers for Disease Control announced that twenty-six homosexual men had died of Kaposi's sarcoma during the previous thirty months, six in California and the others in New York. In September 1982, the CDC used the term "acquired immune deficiency syndrome" (AIDS) to describe the relationship between Kaposi's sarcoma and other opportunistic infections. San Francisco soon became a center for both AIDS infections and responses to the growing crisis.

The University of California, San Francisco (UCSF), the UC system's leading medical center, took a prominent role in research on and treatment for AIDS. San Francisco General Hospital and UCSF professionals developed the San Francisco model of care, emphasizing services for those infected. The San Francisco AIDS Foundation was formed in 1982 to provide services for those infected and to seek an end to the growing epidemic. In 1983, UCSF researchers were centrally involved in discovering the human immunodeficiency virus (HIV), the cause of AIDS.

Researchers identified two groups where the epidemic was most concentrated: men who had sexual relations with men and people who injected illegal drugs. The former group was centered in the Castro district, the latter in the Tenderloin, but both were found throughout much of the city. HIV was not limited to those groups—the virus infected women, heterosexuals, all races, and all ages, including newborn infants whose mothers had HIV. Some people contracted the virus through blood transfusions. By the mid-1990s, many—likely most—San Franciscans knew someone who had died of AIDS.

In 1984, San Francisco was facing a major controversy over the future of the city's twenty to thirty bathhouses and private sex clubs, popular sites where gay men gathered and engaged in sexual relations. By late March, a number of leaders in the gay community, including Harry Britt, who had succeeded Harvey Milk on the Board of Supervisors, urged the temporary closure of the bathhouses and private gay sex clubs, but there was strong opposition as well. Uncertain of the legality of such an action, Mervyn Silverman, the city's public health director, instead proposed to make sex illegal in such places, which *Chronicle* columnist Herb Caen likened to "banning booze in barrooms." The health director finally directed the bathhouses and sex clubs to close in October. In 1988, seeking to combat the spread of HIV/AIDS through contaminated needles used to inject drugs, the city developed a program that permitted drug users to exchange used needles for clean ones.

Despite those efforts, by 1992, AIDS had become the leading cause of death nationwide among men aged twenty-four to forty-four, and San Francisco reached its peaks of 2,648 new cases and 2,332 deaths that year. Thereafter, both the number of new cases and the number of deaths began to decline significantly, as can be seen in figure 9.3. Survival rates increased significantly, as can also be seen on figure 9.3, due especially to the development of antiretroviral therapies.

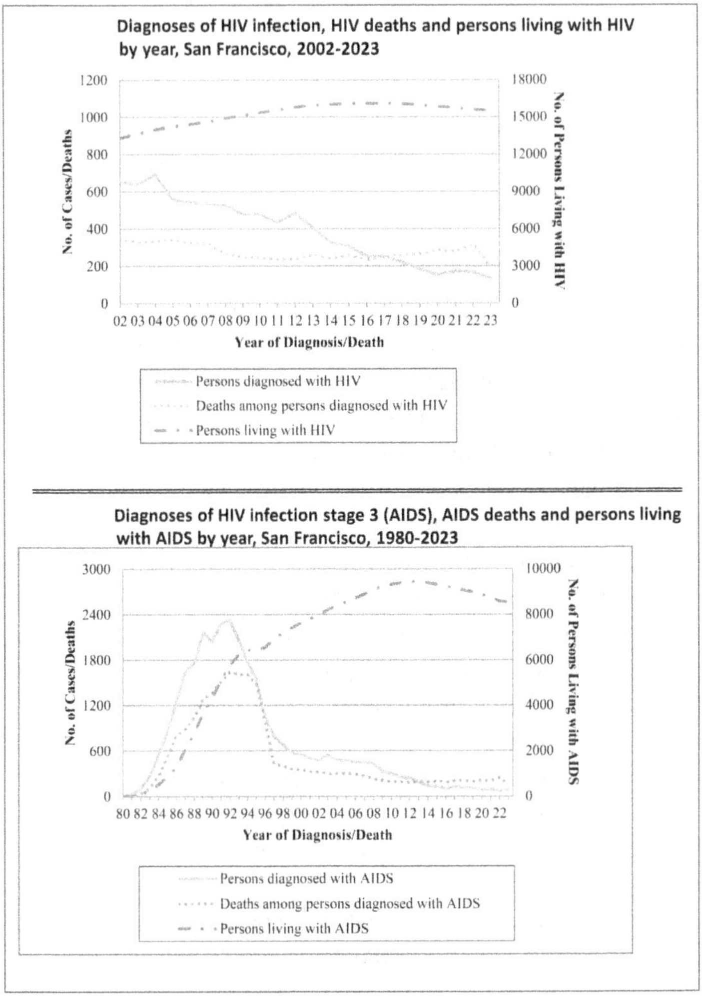

Figure 9.3. HIV and AIDS cases, deaths, and prevalence in San Francisco, 1980–2023. Source: San Francisco Department of Public Health, HIV/AIDS *Epidemiology Annual Report*, 2023.

In 1987, San Franciscans, led by Cleve Jones, created the AIDS Memorial Quilt project, composed of many individual quilts, each a memorial to an individual. The project quickly became nationwide. In October of that year, the Quilt was displayed for the first time on the National Mall in Washington, DC, during the National March on Washington for Lesbian and Gay Rights. Covering a space larger than a football field, it included 1,920 panels. A year later, it was again displayed in Washington, DC, now with 8,288 panels. By 2020, the Quilt had some 50,000 panels. By then, some 700,000 people had died of AIDS in the US including 22,320 in San Francisco. However, by that time, there were also nearly 16,000 people living with AIDS in the city. The city's Department of Public Health continues to work toward its goal of Getting to Zero SF.

The 1989 Earthquake and Its Aftermath

At 5:04 p.m. on October 17, 1989, during the third game of the World Series in San Francisco, between the San Francisco Giants and Oakland Athletics, a magnitude 6.9 earthquake rumbled through the Bay Area. The epicenter was 75 miles south of San Francisco, in Santa Cruz County, on the Loma Prieta section of the San Andreas Fault. The earthquake caused sixty-three deaths, including nine in San Francisco; 3,756 injuries; and significant damage to the built environment. A section of the eastern span of the Bay Bridge collapsed, as did an Oakland freeway. In San Francisco, brick façades fell off many buildings. In the Marina District, where residences had been built on fill land after the PPIE, the ground floor of some apartment buildings collapsed, causing the destruction of the building. A broken gas main there produced the only major fire. The city's fire control system, with its multiple levels of backups, proved equal to the task of stopping the fire. In all, four buildings were destroyed by fire, six collapsed, and sixty-three throughout the city were judged too dangerous to live in.

In the aftermath of the earthquake, several of San Francisco's elevated freeways were found to be too dangerous to remain in use. Two of the stubs of the freeways that had been halted in the 1960s were razed, one that cut through part of the Western Addition and the other that had been built above the Embarcadero. They were not replaced by new freeways, but by new or renovated surface streets. Removing the freeways transformed both neighborhoods. Hayes Valley, west of the Civic Center, blossomed with new restaurants and chic retail stores. The Embarcadero was similarly transformed. Without the freeway, the Ferry Building regained its place as the terminus of Market Street and was renovated with restaurants and retail shops specializing in cuisine. The entire area along the Embarcadero, now sunny much of the time, became a favorite pedestrian walkway.

The construction of BART had included moving the Muni's Market Street lines underground, leaving Market Street for vehicular traffic. In 1973, the Board of Supervisors adopted a transit-first policy, prioritizing mass transit over the automobile. Realizing that tourists enjoyed riding the cable cars, Muni officials began to run historic streetcars on Market Street, eventually designating them as the F line, from Castro Street to the Embarcadero.

City Politics, 1978–2011

The Board of Supervisors had appointed Dianne Feinstein mayor after the assassination of George Moscone, and she was elected in her own right in 1979. In an aftermath to the assassinations, voters amended the charter to return to at-large election of supervisors, making for a more moderate board. As mayor, Feinstein positioned herself as a centrist, supportive of high-rise development downtown and of moderate Democrats nationally. In 1983, however, she proposed banning handguns in San Francisco, which so angered the small, radical White Panther Party that they launched a recall effort. Feinstein easily won with 82 percent of the vote, carrying all but one election precinct. She was easily reelected to another term later that year but did not seek a third term in 1987.

In 1987, Art Agnos, a progressive and an ally of Willie Brown and John Burton, received 70 percent of the vote for mayor, to defeat John Molinari, a former Republican turned moderate Democrat. As mayor, Agnos changed the focus of the Redevelopment Agency from commercial development to housing, disbanded a police unit that had spied on demonstrations, led the way to extending benefits for city employees to domestic partners, and became the first mayor to ride in the annual LGBT Pride Parade. After the 1989 earthquake, he persuaded the Board of Supervisors to remove and not rebuild the two damaged freeways.

In the aftermath of the 1989 earthquake, encampments of homeless people sprang up in several locations, notably on Civic Center Plaza, in front of City Hall. Agnos prohibited the police from removing the encampments until housing could be found, a policy that became a prominent issue in the 1991 mayoral election. Agnos also lost support due to the removal of the Embarcadero Freeway. He narrowly lost to Frank Jordan, a former police chief, and Jordan immediately had the police remove the homeless encampments from Civic Center Plaza.

In 1995, when Jordan came up for reelection, he was defeated by Willie Brown, who had been term-limited out of the California State Assembly by a recently adopted term-limits amendment to the state constitution, an amendment provoked in part by Brown's long tenure as speaker. That same city election in 1995 brought a charter amendment changing the election of supervisors from at large to districts.

Brown served as mayor from 1996 to 2004, when he was term-limited out. A "celebrity mayor," he was featured on national television shows and in national publications. Riding on the dot-com boom and fully supportive of new commercial construction, including a new ballpark for the Giants and the extensive Mission Bay project (see below), Brown oversaw a major reconstruction of City Hall, to improve seismic stability and restore the grandeur of the interior. Serving as mayor during a period of prosperity and growth, Brown was able to secure substantial increases in the city's budget. In addition to a dramatic increase in the number of city employees, Brown's budgets directed hundreds of millions of dollars to addressing homelessness by creating new shelters, supportive housing, and drug treatment centers. But all those efforts failed to reduce homelessness.

In 1997, Brown appointed Gavin Newsom, a successful entrepreneur with investments in restaurants and wineries, to a vacancy on the Board of Supervisors, and Newsom was elected to that seat the next year. He succeeded Brown as mayor after narrowly winning the 2003 election against a more progressive candidate, Matt Gonzalez, a member of the Green Party. Newsom continued Brown's approach of encouraging major development projects, pushed for housing developments on Treasure Island and at Hunters Point, and promoted other projects to reduce homelessness. He was reelected in 2007.

In 2004, Newsom rocketed to national prominence when he directed the county clerk to issue marriage licenses to same-sex couples, in violation of state law. The first couple to be married were Del

Figure 9.4. Del Martin and Phyllis Lyon, celebrating their marriage at City Hall, 2004. Photo by Olga Berrios, courtesy Wikimedia Commons.

Martin and Phyllis Lyon, who had organized the Daughters of Bilitis in 1955. LGBT couples flocked to San Francisco City Hall to be married—some four thousand within a month—coming from throughout the city, the state, and the nation. Across the nation, people contacted San Francisco florists with orders to deliver flowers to any LGBT couple getting married at City Hall. After a month, however, the California Supreme Court ordered the city to stop issuing licenses to same-sex couples and voided the marriages. The city then initiated a court case arguing that denying marriage to same-sex couples violated the state constitution, and the California Supreme Court agreed in 2008. In 2014, the US Supreme Court announced a similar ruling that applied nationwide.

The Continuing Transformation of the Port and SoMa

With the razing of the Embarcadero Freeway, a historic streetcar line was extended along the middle of the Embarcadero from Market Street north to Fisherman's Wharf. Most the piers north of the Ferry Building were renovated. The Exploratorium, an innovative museum for science, technology, and the arts, moved into Pier 15. Other piers housed restaurants or became office or parking space. A new terminal for oceangoing cruise ships opened on Pier 27 in 2014. Some of the warehouses that had once served the northern waterfront were also converted to commercial space or housing; others were razed and replaced with modern structures.

The waterfront south of the Ferry Building underwent even more dramatic transformations. Some derelict piers were demolished, opening vistas of the Bay along the Embarcadero. In 1996, voters approved a plan to construct a new ballpark for the Giants in the China Basin area of the southern waterfront. Construction was completed in 2000. Unlike the previous stadium, no parking was included; instead Muni lines were extended from Market Street along the southern waterfront past the new ballpark to the CalTrain terminal that serves rail lines running south of the city.

When the Port of San Francisco was thriving, the Southern Pacific and Santa Fe railroads had maintained vast railyards on fill land that was once Mission Bay, along the southern waterfront opposite Piers 48–54. With the death of the port as a source of freight, those railyards became obsolete. The Redevelopment Agency planned the conversion of the 303-acre site into a new neighborhood with housing, office buildings, restaurants and shops, a new campus for the University of California, San Francisco, and a new streetcar line, the T line on Third Street, from near the new ballpark to the southern boundary of the city. The UCSF Mission Bay campus opened in 2003 and now includes more than a dozen clinic and research buildings and two hospitals. Other medical and research facilities have located nearby. The Chase Center, an arena for the Golden State Warriors (the professional basketball team) and other events, opened in 2019.

In the aftermath of the 1989 earthquake and demolition of the Embarcadero Freeway, the 1985 Downtown Plan was supplemented by a Transit Center District Plan adopted in 2012. The plan involved demolition of the city's 1939 Transbay Terminal, which had been damaged by the 1989 earthquake. The Transbay Terminal was originally the place where people traveling to and from the East Bay boarded or left interurban rail lines, which converted to buses in 1958. The original plan for the new terminal involved not only bus service, but also the prospect for an underground connection for the CalTrain line that serves commuters to and from the peninsula and perhaps for high-speed rail connections to Southern California. However, the new terminal opened without any rail connections.

A new streetcar line, all underground, extending the T line from the Mission Bay neighborhood to Chinatown, opened in 2022. The early twenty-first century also saw the continuing transformation of SoMa, especially by new companies related to the internet or technology, cementing the city's, and the Bay Area's, standing as a major hub for new technologies. Throughout SoMa, former warehouses and manufacturing sites, made vacant by the death of the port and the exodus of manufacturing, were either converted to new uses or demolished and replaced by new high-rise commercial or residential buildings.

The dramatic changes in the city's economy brought similar changes to existing buildings. The landmark building originally constructed for the Pacific Telephone company in 1925, then the city's tallest building at twenty-six floors, was sold in 2007; the most prominent of its new tenants was Yelp, an internet company that rates businesses. The Merchandise Mart, a large building on Market Street, opened in 1937 to house wholesalers and manufacturers of home furnishings; by 2008 it was nearly empty as a result of changes in that industry. The remodeled and renovated building soon housed Twitter (later renamed X),

Figure 9.5. San Francisco skyline, February 5, 2024, looking east from Twin Peaks. Market Street is in the center, and the twenty-first-century construction in SoMa is to the right (south) of Market Street. The tallest is the Salesforce tower. Photo by Robert W. Cherny.

a social media and social networking company, as its major tenant, but Elon Musk, owner of X, soon moved the company to Texas. Salesforce, an internet-based company providing software and applications for businesses, quickly became one of the largest companies in the world and constructed a sixty-one-story world headquarters building in SoMa, the second-tallest building west of the Mississippi River. Other new skyscrapers nearby transformed the city's skyline, housing such internet giants as Meta (formerly Facebook) as well as many smaller technology-based companies. New or renovated buildings in the area included hotels, apartment buildings, restaurants, and retailers that catered to the thousands of tech employees.

City Politics

Gavin Newsom won election as lieutenant governor in 2010 and resigned as mayor in early 2011. The city charter provides that the Board of Supervisors should fill any vacancy in the office of mayor. The supervisors initially deadlocked, but eventually voted to make Ed Lee mayor. Lee, the city's first Chinese American mayor, had previously served as head of the public works department and as city administrator. Elected in 2011 and reelected in 2015, he died of a heart attack in 2017, and once again the Board of Supervisors choose a mayor. London Breed, a Black woman, was president of the Board of Supervisors and, under the charter, became acting mayor. She sought board support to become mayor, but the board instead chose a caretaker to serve until a special election in June 2018. Breed was then elected and was elected to a full term the following year.

During the mayoralties of Newsom, Lee, and Breed, city politics often involved contests between progressives and moderates, nearly all registered Democrats (and no Republicans), and all, on any national scale, either from the liberal wing of the Democratic party or to its left. As in most other large cities across the country, San Francisco's voters are largely Democrats; Kamala Harris received 80 percent of the city's vote in 2024. John Barbagelata, who left the board in 1979, was the last Republican on that body. However, Barbagelata returned to city politics in the late 1980s, to lead support for a city charter amendment to limit elected city officials to two terms in office, which took effect in 1990. That same year saw voter approval of another charter amendment, to elect supervisors from districts rather than at large.

District election of supervisors seems to guarantee that some members of that board will be progressives and others will be moderates, reflecting the attitudes of the voters in their districts. San Francisco's voters routinely vote on a wide range of policy proposals ranging from new taxes to banning the sale of flavored tobacco. In 2022, analysts for the *San Francisco Chronicle* analyzed fourteen such ballot measures to produce a progressive voter index for each election precinct, then looked at the social and economic characteristics of the progressive and moderate precincts. They found that Black and Asian neighborhoods were the most moderate, Latino neighborhoods were the most progressive, and white neighborhoods showed the greatest range but tended to be more progressive than Black and Asian neighborhoods. The analysts pointed to homeownership as an overlapping variable, with homeowners less likely to vote for tax increases. And homeownership correlates significantly with both Asian and white neighborhoods. However, when it comes to voting for candidates rather than on policies, other factors are also present, notably ethnic or gender identity. For example, progressive candidates with Chinese names have won election in districts with many moderate Chinese voters.

A similar analysis of voting by members of the Board of Supervisors found that the issues that most divided progressives from moderates were the budget, housing policy, and police-related issues. That analysis found three factions during the 2019–21 board term: four progressives, three centrists, and four moderates. However, all but two—one extreme progressive and one extreme moderate—were actually clustered around the political middle, a middle well to left of much of the rest of the country.

In 2019–22, controversy erupted over decisions by the school board, all members of which were considered to be progressives. One decision was to destroy, or permanently cover, thirteen murals at George Washington High School, by Victor Arnautoff, funded by the WPA Fine Arts Project in 1936. One of the murals depicted Washington as a slave owner and another depicted several pioneers marching west past the body of a dead Indigenous warrior, which Arnautoff described as "the march of the white race from the Atlantic to the Pacific." Beginning in 2016, the school district's American Indian Parent Advisory Committee claimed that the depiction of a dead American Indian warrior was offensive, even traumatic, to Indigenous students; others claimed that the depiction of enslaved Black people was offensive to Black students. In June 2019, the school board voted unanimously to paint over all the murals or to cover them with solid panels. The affair drew national attention. Former mayors Willie Brown and Art Agnos opposed the board's decision, as did other prominent figures in the city's political and arts communities. The school's alumni association sued the school district on the grounds that the board's process had violated state law, and in July 2021, a state judge agreed and directed the school board to rescind its action.

By then, the same school board had also voted to change the names of forty-four schools including those named for George Washington, Thomas Jefferson, and Abraham Lincoln, a decision based on a parent committee's research using Wikipedia. The board also voted to convert admission to Lowell High School, the city's competitive academic high school, from merit (based on middle-school GPA) to a lottery, a decision that especially angered members of the city's Asian communities. Both decisions produced lawsuits that the school district lost. In addition, many parents were dissatisfied with the board's handling of student learning during the COVID pandemic.

In a special election in February 2022, voter majorities ranging from 69 to 76 percent recalled the only three school board members eligible for recall. After the recall and appointment of three new board members, the reconstituted board withdrew its appeal of the judge's decision about the murals, ended the renaming controversy, and returned Lowell to its previous admission status.

A few months later, in June 2022, the city's voters, by 55 percent, recalled the district attorney, Chesa Boudin, who had been elected in 2019 as a progressive. He had pledged to reduce the number of incarcerations, eliminate cash bail, reevaluate possible wrongful convictions, and refuse to assist the immigration officers. At the time, the city was experiencing increases in car break-ins, garage burglaries, public drug dealing and drug use, and mass shoplifting by organized groups. Moderate neighborhoods gave the major support to both recalls.

In 2024, for the first time, city elections were combined with federal elections. Kamala Harris, Nancy Pelosi, and all other Democrats seeking federal office received more than 80 percent of the vote. In the nonpartisan elections for city offices, four candidates, all Democrats, dominated the election for mayor. Three professed to be moderates, including the incumbent mayor, London Breed. One, Aaron Peskin, had a reputation as a progressive. In the city's ranked-choice voting process, the redistribution of Peskin's votes gave the victory to Daniel Lurie over Breed. Lurie, a newcomer to politics, is a multigenerational San Franciscan; his stepfather is the great grandnephew of Levi Strauss. In other elections, moderates secured a clear majority on the Board of Supervisors.

Since 1980, San Francisco's always simmering political pot has produced a number of leaders at the state and national level out of proportion to the city's size. At the state level, Willie Brown dominated the state assembly for fifteen years (1980–95), earning a reputation as the most powerful speaker in the state's history. His predecessor as speaker was also a San Franciscan, Leo McCarthy, who then served twelve years as lieutenant governor. John Burton served six years in the California State Assembly, eight years in the California State Senate, including as president pro tempore, and then eight years as head of the state Democratic Party. Fiona Ma moved from the San Francisco Board of Supervisors to the California State Assembly, the State Board of Equalization, and state treasurer. Malia Cohen was elected to the Board of Supervisors in 2010, became president of that board in 2018, and was elected state controller in 2022. Gavin Newsom moved from the Board of Supervisors to mayor, lieutenant governor, and governor. He is known to have presidential ambitions.

Phillip Burton died in 1983 and was succeeded in Congress by his widow, Sala Burton, who died in 1987. Phillip Burton had once recruited Nancy Pelosi to give active support to Democratic candidates, and she became chair of the state Democratic party in 1981. The daughter of a Baltimore mayor, Pelosi was elected to the House of Representatives in 1987 to succeed Sala Burton. Pelosi has held that seat ever

REPUBLICANS HELP TO ELECT WILLIE BROWN SPEAKER OF THE ASSEMBLY, 1980

Born in Mineola, Texas, a rigidly segregated town, Willie Brown worked shining shoes and as a janitor while attending the segregated schools. He left Mineola after graduating from high school, came to San Francisco, graduated from San Francisco State College, and then from law school. Elected to the California State Assembly in 1964, he was repeatedly re-elected. In 1974, after running unsuccessfully for speaker, he remained in the assembly but focused on his law practice.

He became known for his flamboyance, including his fast cars—Porsches, which he usually drove every day over the ninety miles between his home in San Francisco and the capitol in Sacramento. He was also known for his stylish suits and his often barbed sense of humor. He once said, "Dressing is a matter of taste, and I've met very few Republicans with good taste."

In 1980, some Democrats in the California State Assembly sought to deny another term as Speaker to Leo McCarthy, a San Franciscan. Their candidate was Howard Berman. Democrats in the assembly, and in the state more generally, divided sharply between Berman's supporters, mostly in Southern California, and McCarthy's.

When McCarthy withdrew as a candidate, Brown immediately became the major opponent to Berman. When the majority Democrats split evenly between Berman and Brown, the minority Republicans approached Brown. He cut a deal, Republicans voted for Brown, and he won.

Brown joked, "The little black kid can count." And he joked that Berman and McCarthy had each spent millions of dollars backing assembly candidates in the fall elections, but "I spent $80,000, with $40,000 on clothes, and I won."

The Republicans' assembly leader later explained, "We really believed that Willie would self-destruct... We really felt that Willie's flamboyant approach would get him into so much trouble with his own caucus that he wouldn't last. And we were certainly wrong."

Brown remained as speaker for the next fifteen years, the longest tenure of any speaker in the state's history. Generally acknowledged as the most powerful speaker in the state's history, he called himself "the Ayatollah of the Assembly."

In the end, Brown had to leave the assembly when voters amended the state constitution to place term limits on elected state officials. He then brought his flamboyance to two terms as mayor of San Francisco, during which he called himself "Da Mayor."

since, notching several firsts in House leadership, most significantly the first woman to serve as speaker, from which post she steered crucial legislation to approval, notably the Affordable Care Act in 2010.

After Dianne Feinstein served as mayor (1978–88), she lost as candidate for governor in 1990, but in 1992 became the first woman from California to be elected to the US Senate. Reelected five times, she served for thirty-one years before her death in 2023, becoming the longest serving senator from California. In the Senate, she held significant leadership positions on major committees, and authored important legislation (since expired) to ban assault weapons.

Kamala Harris was elected San Francisco district attorney in 2003, then California attorney general, US senator, and vice president of the United States, becoming the first woman and first person of color to hold that office. In 2024, she was the unsuccessful Democratic candidate for president.

NANCY PELOSI DEFINES "SAN FRANCISCO VALUES," 2006

Bill O'Reilly, once a commentator for Fox News, has claimed that he coined the phrase "San Francisco values" as a pejorative term, a way to demean progressives. The term became especially widespread among conservative pundits and politicians after the 2006 midterm elections, when Nancy Pelosi, a member of Congress from San Francisco, was about to become the first woman to serve as the speaker of the House of Representatives. A Georgia newspaper warned, "Pelosi will be speaker and her far-left San Francisco values—gay marriage, cutting and running from Iraq, coddling terrorists, raising taxes, amnesty for illegals—will become the House agenda."

Pelosi embraced the term "San Francisco values" and offered her own definition: "It is my honor to represent our City and our San Francisco values in the Congress: jobs with dignity, human rights, reproductive justice, LGBTQ equality, respect for immigrants, and care for our planet and for each other." She has often added, echoing Phoebe Apperson Hearst and other woman suffrage advocates from more than a century before, "When people ask me 'What are the three most important issues facing the Congress?' I always say 'our children; our children; our children'—their health, their education, the housing and economic security of their families, a clean safe environment where they can thrive, and a world in peace where all are welcome and can reach their fulfillment."

Twenty-First Century Medical Crisis: The COVID Pandemic and After

Late in 2019, a new virus, soon labeled COVID-19 for Corona Virus Disease 2019, appeared in Wuhan, China. It soon spread worldwide, becoming a pandemic. Between early 2020 and September 2023, some one hundred million cases were recorded in the US, and more than one million deaths. San Francisco recorded more than two hundred thousand cases and 1,237 deaths, as can be seen in figure 9.6.

In San Francisco, Mayor Breed declared a state of emergency on February 25, 2020. Health officers from around the Bay Area cooperated on public safety measures, notably a shelter-in-place order that required nonessential businesses, including schools, libraries, and museums, to close and residents to remain at home except for essential needs. Schools from kindergarten through university scrambled to convert to remote classes. San Francisco joined other Bay Area cities and counties in issuing a mask mandate—requiring residents to wear masks when out of their homes. By the fall, some businesses were allowed to reopen. With a major surge in infections in early 2021, efforts continued to require masking and to stay at home. When it became clear that transmission of the virus was much less likely outside, many San Francisco restaurants quickly added outdoor dining spots by erecting floors and walls in the parking places in front of their businesses.

After vaccines became available in December 2020, San Franciscans rushed to line up. By July 2021, more than 600,000 San Franciscans had received their first vaccinations, and by September 2023 the number reached 770,000—nearly 90 percent of the population and one of the highest rates in the nation. With declining numbers of new cases and increasing proportions of vaccinated residents, businesses, schools, and other public places reopened. The mandates issued in the early phases of the pandemic seem to have reduced the number of infections and the death rate.

The COVID pandemic nonetheless had a serious effect in the city. The city's population in 2020 was 870,014, and was estimated to be 807,774 in 2022, a 7 percent decline. Some, perhaps many, of those leaving during the COVID pandemic were among the wealthier residents, who could afford to relocate. Many of the internet and technology companies either permitted or required their employees to work from home. Committees and boards met virtually. Much of that continued after the restrictions were lifted. By mid-2024, San Francisco had the highest office vacancy rate, at 37 percent, of any major US city. Downtown restaurants, bars, and shops saw a sharp decline in customers, and many closed permanently. Retail stores, especially those that had been hit repeatedly by organized shoplifting, also closed. Some owners of downtown buildings were unable to pay their mortgages, and lenders took title.

Amid the closings and foreclosures, homeless encampments multiplied on city streets, and, in 2022, a federal court order blocked efforts to remove them unless alternative housing was offered. During the early 2020s, five hundred to seven hundred tents were scattered along San Francisco's sidewalks, under freeways, and elsewhere. Surveys found some eight thousand homeless individuals, half without shelter. The homeless were disproportionately Black (35 percent), Latino (30 percent), and LGBT (28 percent). Half were relative newcomers to the city, rather than long-term residents, and half were addicted to alcohol or drugs. In 2024, the US Supreme Court reversed the earlier court decision prohibiting local governments from removing homeless encampments, and Mayor Breed directed the police to move aggressively to remove encampments. But homelessness continued and was an issue in Breed's defeat in the 2024 election.

During the early 2020s, and sometimes among the homeless encampments, open-air drug markets thrived, especially in the Tenderloin and parts of the Mission, and open-air drug use, especially of fentanyl, became a common sight in many parts of the city, especially in the encampments. Deaths from drug overdoses, mostly from fentanyl, surged, totaling more than two thousand between 2020 and 2024; nearly a third of those who died had no fixed address. Drug addiction fed the crime rate, which included large-scale shoplifting, break-ins, burglaries, and theft. Car break-ins, typically of rental cars with tourists' luggage inside, multiplied, with more than 1,600 reports per month in mid-2023—and more not reported because of the cumbersome reporting process. A poll in mid-2023 found that 48 percent

Deaths by month

COVID-19 deaths are shown below. Deaths are shown on the date the individual died.

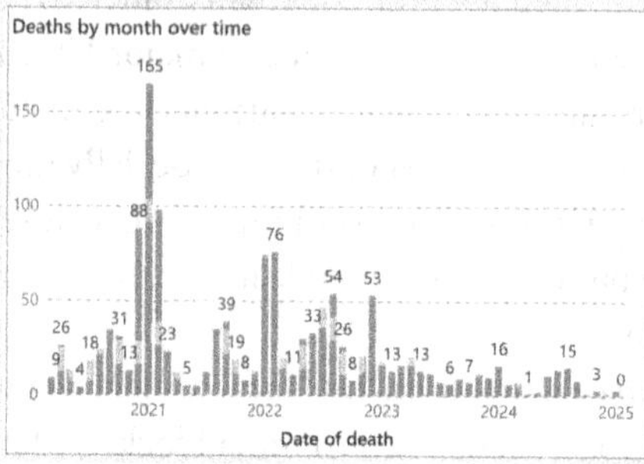

Monthly and cumulative deaths

Month	Deaths	Cumulative deaths	Data reliability
February 2025	0	1,380	Less reliable, updates are likely
January 2025	3	1,380	Less reliable, updates are likely
December 2024	1	1,377	Less reliable, updates are likely
November 2024	3	1,376	More reliable
October 2024	1	1,373	More reliable
September 2024	8	1,372	More reliable

City and County of San Francisco
Data through 2/11/2025
Updated weekly

Total COVID-19 deaths in San Francisco

The total cumulative number of deaths is the running total. The cumulative total will always increase. The steeper increases show times with more frequent deaths.

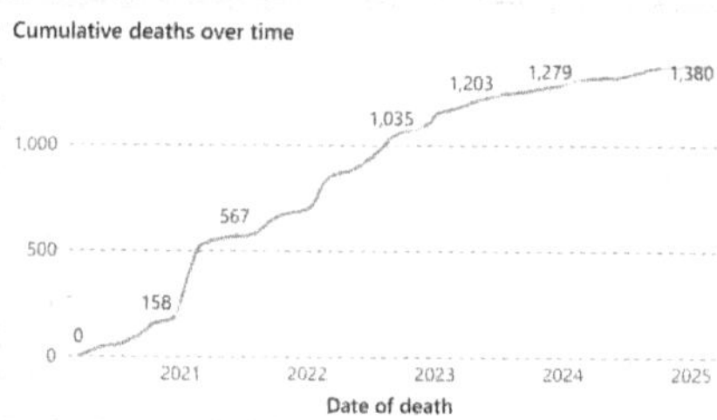

Cumulative deaths by day

Date	New deaths	Cumulative deaths
2/11/2025	0	1,380
2/10/2025	0	1,380
2/9/2025	0	1,380
2/8/2025	0	1,380

City and County of San Francisco
Data through 2/11/2025
Updated weekly

Figure 9.6. Deaths from COVID in San Francisco. Source: San Francisco Department of Public Health.

of respondents nationwide thought that San Francisco was a "dangerous" place to live or work, a response similar to those for Washington, DC, and Atlanta. By 2024, however, the crime rate had dropped significantly, especially for car break-ins.

Some prognosticators foresaw a "doom loop" in which downtown business closings led to more closings. Others, more optimistic, nonetheless predicted a long recovery. But among the gloom, there were some hopeful signs. The corporation developing the long-vacant site of Schlage Lock announced plans for a new, carbon-neutral community with ten thousand homes and twenty thousand jobs. A major company opened a large new store in the downtown area. An investment company announced it was buying seventy-five apartment buildings then in foreclosure.

Over all such plans hung the ever more pressing reality of climate change. City and state governments have promoted electric vehicles and residential solar panels to reduce carbon emissions, and both are now common sights in the city. Given projections of sea-level rise, city officials laid plans to protect low-lying areas along the Bay including much of the fill land (see map 1.1 for the original shorelines) and the recently developed housing on Treasure Island. Long-term subsidence of fill land complicated such planning.

Amid the many overlapping crises and ambitious plans for a different future, the city's incredible natural beauty remains, and life in most of its residential neighborhoods goes on much as it always has.

Select Bibliography

In researching San Francisco history, daily newspapers are important starting points. The *Chronicle*, *Examiner*, and *Call*; some others from the nineteenth century; and more recent neighborhood newspapers are available online, as are San Francisco city directories. The San Francisco History Center at the main branch of the San Francisco Public Library, the Labor Archives at San Francisco State University, the California Historical Society Collection at Stanford, and the Bancroft Library at the University of California, Berkeley, all hold important primary sources.

There are many books and articles about San Francisco. The following selection is an effort to list works that I've used in preparing this book or that I consider important.

Ackley, Laura A. *San Francisco's Jewel City: The Panama-Pacific International Exposition of 1915*. Heyday, 2015.

Bean, Walton. *Boss Ruef's San Francisco: The Story of the Union Labor Party, Big Business, and the Graft Prosecution*. University of California Press, 1952.

Beebe, Rose Marie, and Robert M. Senkewicz. *Junipero Serra: California, Indians, and the Transformation of a Missionary*. University of Oklahoma Press, 2015.

Beebe, Rose Marie, and Robert M. Senkewicz. *Mariano Guadalupe Vallejo: Life in Spanish, Mexican, and American California*. University of Oklahoma Press, 2023.

Berglund, Barbara. *Making San Francisco American: Cultural Frontiers in the Urban West, 1846–1906*. University Press of Kansas, 2007.

Blackford, Mansel G. *The Lost Dream: Businessmen and City Planning on the Pacific Coast, 1890–1920*. Ohio State University Press, 1993.

Boyd, Nan Alamilla. *Wide Open Town: A History of Queer San Francisco to 1965*. University of California Press, 2003.

Brandi, Richard. *Garden Neighborhoods of San Francisco: The Development of Residence Parks, 1905–1924*. McFarland & Company, 2021.

Brechin, Gray. *Imperial San Francisco: Urban Power, Earthly Ruin*. University of California Press, 1999.

Brechin, Gray. "Politics and Modernism: The Trial of the Rincon Annex Murals." In *On the Edge of America: California Modernist Art, 1900–1950*, edited by Paul J. Karlstrom. University of California Press, 1996.

Broussard, Albert S. *Black San Francisco: The Struggle for Racial Equality in the West, 1900–1954*. University Press of Kansas, 1993.

Bullough, William A. *The Blind Boss and His City: Christopher Augustine Buckley and Nineteenth-Century San Francisco*. University of California Press, 1979.

Carlsson, Chris, and LisaRuth Elliott, eds. *Ten Years That Shook the City: San Francisco 1968–1978*. City Lights Books, 2011.

Chen, Yong. *Chinese San Francisco, 1850–1943: A Trans-Pacific Community*. Stanford University Press, 2000.

Chandler, Arthur, and Marvin Nathan. *The Fantastic Fair: The Story of the California Midwinter International Exposition, Golden Gate Park, San Francisco, 1894*. Pogo Press, 1994.

Cherny, Robert W. "City Commercial, City Beautiful, City Practical: The San Francisco Visions of William C. Ralston, James D. Phelan, and Michael M. O'Shaughnessy." *California History* 73 (1994/95): 296–307.

Cherny, Robert W. "The Controversy at Coit Tower, 1934." *The Argonaut* 28 (Summer 2017): 68–91.

Cherny, Robert W. "The International Context of Two US Supreme Court Decisions: *Schneiderman v. U.S.* (1943) and *Yates v. U.S.* (1957)." *Siècles, la revue du centre d'histoire espaces et cultures*, no. 58a (2025).

Cherny, Robert W. "Longshoremen of San Francisco Bay, 1849–1960." In *Dock Workers: International Explorations in Comparative Labor History, 1790–1970* [conference proceedings], ed. Sam Davies et al. 2 vols. Ashgate Publishing, Ltd., 2000. I:102–40.

Cherny, Robert W. "Patterns of Toleration and Discrimination in San Francisco: Civil War to World War I." *California History* 73 (1994): 130–41.

Cherny, Robert W. "San Francisco's New-Deal Murals in Long-Term Perspective: Controversy, Neglect, and Restoration." *California History* 97 (February 2020): 3–32.

Cherny, Robert W. *The Coit Tower Murals: New Deal Art and Political Controversy in San Francisco*. University of Illinois Press, 2024.
Cherny, Robert W. *Harry Bridges: Labor Radical, Labor Legend*. University of Illinois Press, 2023.
Cherny, Robert W. *San Francisco Reds: Communists in the San Francisco Bay Area, 1919–1958*. University of Illinois Press, 2024.
Cherny, Robert W. *Victor Arnautoff and the Politics of Art*. University of Illinois Press, 2017.
Cherny, Robert W., and William Issel. *San Francisco: Presidio, Port, and Pacific Metropolis*. Boyd and Fraser Publishing Company, 1981.
Cherny, Robert W., Gretchen Lemke Santangelo, and Richard Griswold del Castillo. *Competing Visions: A History of California*. Houghton Mifflin, 2005. 2nd ed.: Wadsworth, 2014.
Cherny, Robert W., Ann Marie Wilson, and Mary Ann Irwin, eds. *California Women and Politics: From the Gold Rush to the Great Depression*. University of Nebraska Press, 2011.
Clary, Raymond H. *The Making of Golden Gate Park: The Early Years, 1865–1906*. California Living Books, 1980.
Clary, Raymond H. *The Making of Golden Gate Park, 1906–1950*. Don't Call It Frisco Press, 1987.
Contreras, Eduardo. *Latinos and the Liberal City: Politics and Protest in San Francisco*. University of Pennsylvania Press, 2019.
Corbett, Michael R. *Port City: The History and Transformation of the Port of San Francisco, 1848–2010*. San Francisco Architectural Heritage, 2010.
Cordova, Cary. *The Heart of the Mission: Latino Art and Politics in San Francisco*. University of Pennsylvania Press, 2017.
Daniels, Douglas Henry. *Pioneer Urbanites: A Social and Cultural History of Black San Francisco*. Temple University Press, 1980.
DeLeon, Richard Edward. *Left Coast City: Progressive Politics in San Francisco, 1975–1991*. University Press of Kansas, 1992.
Englander, Susan. *Class Coalition and Class Conflict in the California Woman Suffrage Movement, 1907–1912: The San Francisco Wage Earners' Suffrage League*. Edwin Mellen Press, 1992.
Federal Writers Project of the Works Progress Administration of Northern California. *San Francisco in the 1930s: The WPA Guide to the City by the Bay*. Reprint, University of California Press, 2011.
Fortunate Eagle, Adam. *Alcatraz! Alcatraz! The Indian Occupation of 1969–1971*. Heyday Books, 1992.

Fradkin, Philip L. *The Great Earthquake and Firestorms of 1906: How San Francisco Nearly Destroyed Itself*. University of California Press, 2005.
Frost, Richard J. *The Mooney Case: The San Francisco Preparedness Day Bombing of 1916 and Its Aftermath*. Stanford University Press, 1967.
Gumina, Deanna Paoli. *The Italians of San Francisco, 1850–1930*. Center for Migration Studies, 1978.
Hansen, Gladys C., and Emmet Condon. *Denial of Disaster: The Untold Story and Photographs of the San Francisco Earthquake and Fire of 1906*. Ed. David Fowler. Cameron and Co., 1989.
Hartman, Chester, et al. *City for Sale: The Transformation of San Francisco*. University of California Press, 2002.
Hennings, Robert E. *James D. Phelan and the Wilson Progressives of California*. Garland Publishing, 1985.
Hudson, Lynn M. *West of Jim Crow: The Fight Against California's Color Line*. University of Illinois Press, 2020.
Irwin, Mary Ann. "'Going About and Doing Good': The Politics of Benevolence, Welfare, and Gender in San Francisco, 1850–1880." *Pacific Historical Review* 68 (1999): 365–96.
Issel, William. *Church and State in the City: Catholics and Politics in Twentieth-Century San Francisco*. Temple University Press, 2012.
Issel, William. *For Both Cross and Flag: Catholic Action, Anti-Catholicism, and National Security in World War II San Francisco*. Temple University Press, 2010.
Issel, William. "Land Values, Human Values, and Preservation of the City's Treasured Appearance: Environmentalism, Politics, and the San Francisco Freeway Revolt." *Pacific Historical Review* 68 (1999): 611–46.
Issel, William. "New Deal and Wartime Origins of San Francisco's Postwar Political Culture: The Case of Growth Politics and Policy." In *The Way We Really Were: The Golden State in the Second World War*, ed. by Roger W. Lotchin. University of Illinois Press, 2000.
Issel, William, and Robert W. Cherny. *San Francisco, 1865–1932: Politics, Power, and Urban Development*. University of California Press, 1986.
Jacobs, John. *A Rage for Justice: The Passion and Politics of Phillip Burton*. University of California Press, 1995.
Kahn, Judd. *Imperial San Francisco: Politics and Planning in an American City, 1897–1906*. University of Nebraska Press, 1979.
Kazin, Michael. *Barons of Labor: The San Francisco Building Trades and Union Power in the Progressive Era*. University of Illinois Press, 1989.

King, John. *Portal: San Francisco's Ferry Building and the Reinvention of American Cities*. W. W. Norton, 2024.

Kinkead, Gwen. *Chinatown: A Portrait of a Closed Society*. Harper Collins, 1992.

Lapp, Rudolph. *Archy Lee: A California Fugitive Slave Case*. Book Club of California, 1969. Reprint, Heyday Books, 2008.

Lemke-Santangelo, Gretchen. *Daughters of Aquarius: Women of the Sixties Counterculture*. University of Kansas Press, 2009.

Lotchin, Roger. *San Francisco, 1846–1856: From Hamlet to City*. Oxford University Press, 1974.

Low, Victor. *The Unimpressible Race: A Century of Educational Struggle by the Chinese in San Francisco*. East-West Publishing Company, Inc., 1982,

Margolin, Malcolm. *The Ohlone Way: Indian Life in the San Francisco-Monterey Bay Area*. Rev. ed. Heyday Books, 2014.

Matthews, Glenna. *The Golden State in the Civil War: Thomas Starr King, the Republican Party, and the Birth of Modern California*. Cambridge University Press, 2012.

Matthews, Glenna. *Silicon Valley, Women, and the California Dream: Gender, Class, and Opportunity in the Twentieth Century*. Stanford University Press, 2003.

Milliken, Randall, Laurence H. Shoup, and Beverley R. Ortiz. *Ohlone/Costanoan Indians of the San Francisco Peninsula and Their Neighbors, Yesterday and Today*. National Park Service, Golden Gate National Recreation Area, 2009.

Mitchell, Lincoln A. *San Francisco Year Zero: Political Upheaval, Punk Rock, and a Third-Place Baseball Team*. Rutgers University Press, 2020.

Mitchell, Lincoln A. *Three Years Our Mayor: George Moscone and the Making of Modern San Francisco*. University of Nevada Press, 2025.

Mullen, Kevin J. *Let Justice Be Done: Crime and Politics in Early San Francisco*. University of Nevada Press, 1989.

Mullins, William H. *The Depression and the Urban West Coast, 1929–1933: Los Angeles, San Francisco, Seattle, and Portland*. Indiana University Press, 1991.

Narell, Irena. *Our City: The Jews of San Francisco*. Howell-North Books, 1981.

Ngai, Mae. *The Lucky Ones: One Family and the Extraordinary Invention of Chinese America*. Houghton Mifflin Harcourt, 2010.

Nickliss, Alexandra M. *Phoebe Apperson Hearst: A Life of Power and Politics*. University of Nebraska Press, 2017.

Paddison, Joshua. "Summers of Worry, Summers of Defiance: San Franciscans for Academic Freedom and Education and the Bay Area Opposition to HUAC, 1959–1960." *California History* 78 (1999): 188–201, 219–21.

Pepin, Elizabeth, and Lewis Watts. *Harlem of the West: The San Francisco Fillmore Jazz Era*. Chronicle Books, 2006.

Richardson, James. *Willie Brown: A Biography*. University of California Press, 1996.

Richardson, Peter. *No Simple Highway: A Cultural History of the Grateful Dead*. St. Martin's Press, 2015.

Saxton, Alexander. *The Indispensable Enemy: Labor and the Anti-Chinese Movement in California*. University of California Press, 1995.

Selvin, David. *A Terrible Anger: The 1934 Maritime and General Strikes in San Francisco*. Wayne State University Press, 1998.

Selvin, Joel. *The Haight: Love, Rock, and Revolution*. Insight Editions, 2014.

Senkewicz, Robert. *Vigilantes in Gold Rush San Francisco*. Stanford University Press, 1985.

Shaken, Andrew M. *Into the Void Pacific: Building the 1939 San Francisco World's Fair*. University of California Press, 2014.

Shilts, Randy. *And the Band Played On: Politics, People, and the AIDS Epidemic*. St. Martin's Press, 1987.

Shilts, Randy. *The Mayor of Castro Street: The Life and Times of Harvey Milk*. St. Martin's Press, 1982.

Sides, Josh. *Erotic City: Sexual Revolutions and the Making of Modern San Francisco*. Oxford University Press, 2009.

Stryker, Susan, and Jim Van Buskirk. *Gay by the Bay: A History of Queer Culture in the San Francisco Bay Area*. Chronicle Books, 1996.

Summers Sandoval, Tomás. *Latinos at the Golden Gate: Creating Community and Identity in San Francisco*. University of North Carolina Press, 2013.

Talbot, David. *Season of the Witch: Enchantment, Terror, and Deliverance in the City of Love*. Free Press, 2012.

Taper, Bernard. *Mark Twain's San Francisco*. Harper and Row, 1963.

Tobriner, Stephen. *Bracing for Disaster: Earthquake-Resistant Architecture and Engineering in San Francisco, 1838–1933*. Heyday Books and the Bancroft Library, University of California, Berkeley, 2006.

Tygiel, Jules. *Workingmen in San Francisco, 1880–1901*. Garland, 1992.

Walsh, James P., and Timothy J. O'Keefe. *Legacy of a Native Son: James Duval Phelan and Villa Montalvo*. Forbes Mill Press, 1993.

Wels, Susan. *San Francisco: Arts for the City: Civic Art and Urban Change, 1932–2012*. Heyday Books for San Francisco Arts Commission, 2013.

White, Richard. *Who Killed Jane Stanford? A Gilded Age Tale of Murder, Deceit, Spirits, and the Birth of a University*. W.W. Norton & Company, 2022.

Wirt, Frederick M. *Power in the City: Decision Making in San Francisco*. University of California Press, 1974.

Yonada, Karl. *Ganbatte: Sixty-Year Struggle of a Kibei Worker*. UCLA Asian American Studies Center, 1983.

Young, Terence. *Building San Francisco's Parks, 1850–1930*. Johns Hopkins University Press, 2004.

Yung, Judy. *Unbound Feet: A Social History of Chinese Women in San Francisco*. University of California Press, 1995.

In addition to these books and articles, the San Francisco Planning Department has put several historic context statements (HCSS) online, at https://sfplanning.org/project/citywide-historic-context-statement#completed. I've found the following especially useful:

Architectural Resources Group. "Historic Context Statement: The Panama-Pacific International Exposition and the Development of the Marina District." 2023.

Graves, Donna. "Citywide Historic Context Statement for Counterculture (1965–1975)." 2024.

Graves, Donna, and Shayne Watson. "Citywide Historic Context Statement for Lesbian, Gay, Bisexual, Transgender, and Queer History in San Francisco." 2016.

San Francisco Planning Department. "City Within a City: Historic Context Statement for San Francisco's Mission District." 2007.

VerPlanck, Christopher, et al. "African American Citywide Historic Context Statement." 2024.

VerPlanck, Christopher, and Donna Graves. "San Francisco New Deal Historic Context Statement: Rebuilding the City, 1933 to 1943." 2023.

I've also benefited from reviewing some Historic Content Statements still in progress and not yet online, especially the Pan-Latino and Residential Parks Historic Content Statements. They are likely to be available at the website above in the near future.

Index

About the Author

ROBERT W. CHERNY is professor emeritus of history at San Francisco State University. He has written extensively on the history of San Francisco, including, most recently, *The Coit Tower Murals: New Deal Art and Political Controversy in San Francisco*. He is also coauthor with William Issel of *San Francisco, 1865–1932: Politics, Power, and Urban Development*. He has been a National Endowment for the Humanities fellow, Distinguished Fulbright Lecturer at Moscow State University, Visiting Research Scholar at the University of Melbourne, and Senior Fulbright Scholar at Heidelberg University. He served for five years on San Francisco's Landmarks Preservation Advisory Board and continues to be involved in historic preservation activities in the city.